you gave me a wide place

you gave me a wide place

holy places of our lives

For Dr Sonya Williams!
Thank you for all
you do at Eden,
Blessings,
Paul Stroble
6/21

paul e. stroble

UPPER ROOM BOOKS®
NASHVILLE

You Gave Me a Wide Place: *Holy Places of Our Lives*

Cover and interior design: Christa Schoenbrodt / Studio Haus
Cover photos: Tree—Teri Dixon/Getty Images; Cross—Mel Curtis/Getty Images
Typesetting: PerfecType / Nashville
First printing: 2006

Library of Congress Cataloging-in-Publication Data

Stroble, Paul E.,
You gave me a wide place : holy places of our lives / by Paul E. Stroble.
p. cm.
Includes bibliographical references.
ISBN-13: 978-0-8358-1002-9
1. Sacred space. 2. Spiritual life—Christianity. I. Title.
BL580.S775 2006
263'.042—dc22 2006028499

Printed in the United States of America

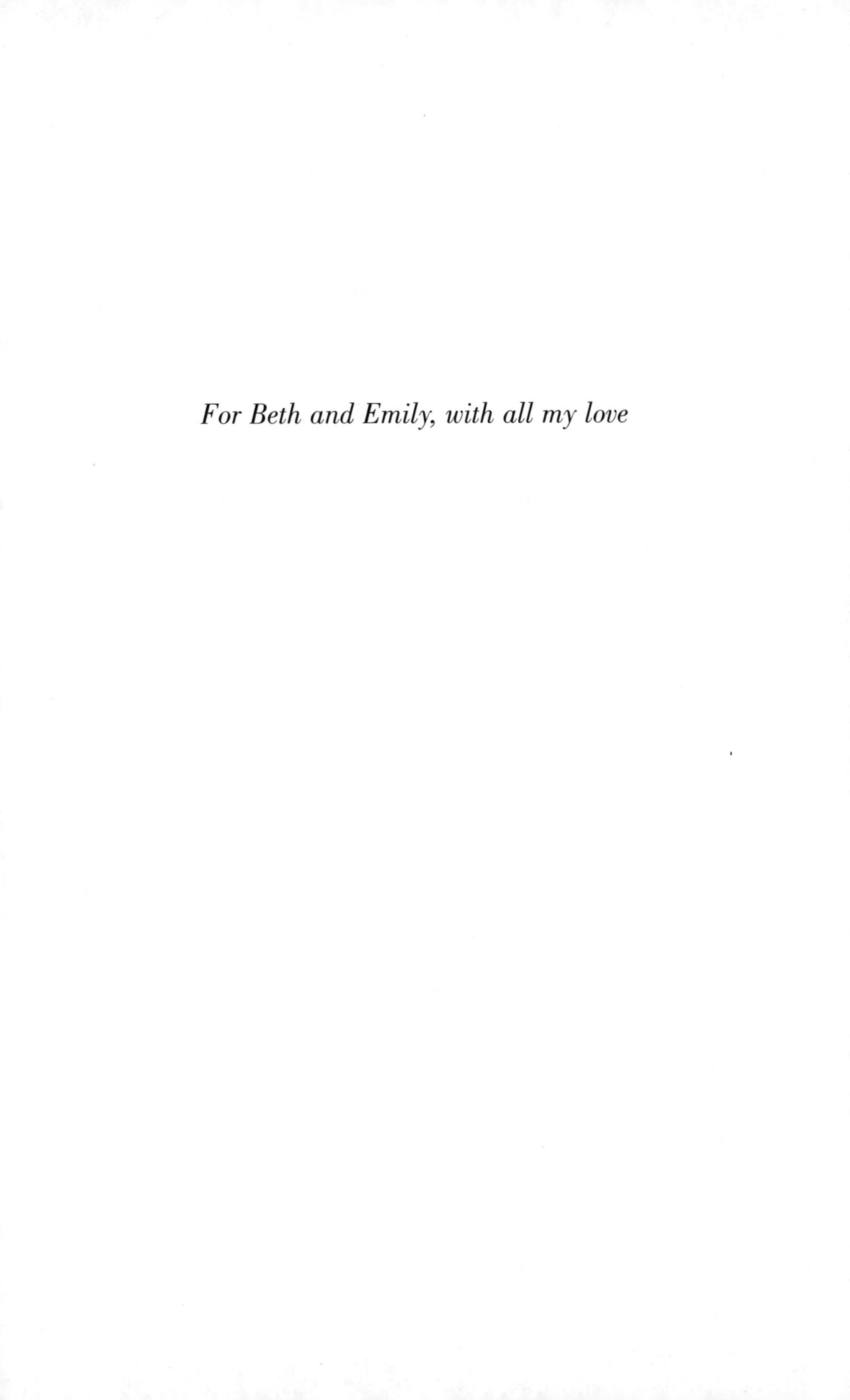

For Beth and Emily, with all my love

contents

acknowledgments

My grateful thanks go to several friends who helped with this project: Karen Jordan Allen, Martina Bowling, Judy Baumann, Tammy Chappel, Sylvia Chinn-Levy, Jim Coleman, Duane Covrig, Tom Dukes, Julie Galambush, Steve Hallam, Linda Hanabarger, Tom Hannon, Cara Kelly, Susan Kirkpatrick, KB Kleckner, Malcolm Mackey, Bev McAdams, Jim McClaren, Marianne Mercer, Brenda Baptist Protz, Paula Ritchie, Kym Rohrbach, Michael Tanner, Mary Townsend, Dick Williams, Victor Wilson, Stacey Wojtowicz, and William Woodall. None of them is responsible for my reflections, but their stories and descriptions have been indispensable for this book and I appreciate their time and generosity. I also thank JoAnn Miller and Jeannie Crawford-Lee of Upper Room Books, Mary Ann Elam, Keith Sculle, Coco's Coffee Bar, and the Basement Bible Bunch class at Montrose Zion United Methodist Church in Montrose, Ohio. My appreciation also goes to my family: my mother,

Mildred Stroble, who shares in this book through our common memories; Beth and Emily, to whom this book is dedicated, for their constant love, help, and encouragement; and the cats Domino and Odd Ball, for their special love.

Some of the material about my hometown first appeared in the magazine *Springhouse* (Herod, IL), and later in my book *Journeys Home: Thoughts and Places* (Louisville, KY, 1995). My thanks go to Gary and Judy DeNeal, *Springhouse* editors, for publishing this material in its original form.

I'd also like to thank the Louisville Institute for the Study of Protestantism and American Culture, and the director, James W. Lewis, for the Institute's generous Religious Leaders grant in 1995. My research project concerned church leadership and volunteer ministries, and I've been able to use that research again in chapter 5 of this book.

introduction

My hometown is Vandalia, Illinois—population: seven thousand—an hour east of St. Louis, Missouri. Vandalia's central business district lies along Gallatin Street, where the old state capitol also stands. When Petula Clark's song "Downtown" hit the charts in 1964, I was seven, and I fancied that the song pertained to a place like my hometown with its busy stores and bright lights. I loved the clothing shops, restaurants, appliance stores, drugstores, and downtown groceries. I remember delicious hamburgers served at Andy's Café, cherry Cokes from Cain's Drugstore, and gumball machines inside Reeve's Barbershop. My other fond recollections include the wooden bins of tools inside Greer hardware store, the hand-drawn price signs on the Tri-City Grocery shelves, and my cousin's photography and gift shop.

North of Gallatin on Fifth Street stands my childhood church: First Christian. I loved downtown—the fun, social place where my parents and

I shopped—and geographically speaking (we lived several blocks north) going to church was going downtown. Geography and theology sentimentally mixed in my mind at an early age.

The church was not especially old, but to a small child the building seemed as old and lofty as the Most High. Inside and out, the church filled my childish imagination with a thrilling sense of mystery. The hymn board, crafted of dark wood, held black cardboard numbers—bold and ominous. The altar announced peremptorily, "This Do in Remembrance of Me." It might as well have said, "I am the great and powerful Oz." I believed the Holy of Holies lived right there, invisibly, as if concealed in the darkness of the wood, in the blackness of the cardboard numbers, waiting for the moment to come and judge us all.

Even the hymns within the pages of well-used hymnals contained spiritual mysteries and syntactical puzzles, for the meanings of some of the hymn lyrics were broken up and confused by the accents of the music: "Remold them, make us, like thee, divine." *Try to structure* that *sentence*, I thought! Then there was the Old Hundredth:

> Praise him all creatures here below,
> Praise him above, ye heavenly host.

I was young and didn't "get it." If we praise him above the heavenly host, then how do we get up there? What kind of "creatures" are referred to? Scary creatures? If the song said, "Everyone down here: praise him!" I'd have understood perfectly.

a sacred place

As I grew older, I associated the church with happy occasions, such as our Halloween canvasses for UNICEF and annual Christmas programs. During vacation Bible school, I felt the joy of summer mingling with the happiness of a new discovery about the God who is love. On peaceful Sunday mornings, the minister preached about mansions, flowing streams, hills, solid rocks, and people who lived off the land. Such things I already understood from living in Southern Illinois!

> I lift up my eyes to the hills—
> from where will my help come?
> My help comes from the Lord,
> who made heaven and earth. (Psalm 121:1-2)

The cadences of Hebrew poetry seemed appropriate for this small-town kingdom of God just off Interstate 70.

Throughout the year, our biblical stories were children's tales about animals and smiling people, told in small rooms stocked with colorful literature, tiny chairs, paste, and bright-hued pencils and papers. Our Sunday school teachers faithfully taught us kids.

Sunday school gave me a strong sense of both grace and place. We met downstairs in the church fellowship hall, with its muted paint, upright piano, and folding doors separating the children's Sunday school rooms. The comfortable downstairs calls forth a positive feeling about my childhood church, in spite of the imagined apocalyptic look of the sanctuary and the terrors of having to recite Old Testament books by heart. The old pictures on the walls—especially familiar renderings of Sallman's "Head of Christ"—bespoke constancy beyond the ambiguities of life. The well-used hymnals and maps of the Holy Land had the same imaginative effect: the latter seemed as wonderful to me as the crumpled highway maps my Dad kept in the car glove compartment.

Our Sunday school literature contained monochrome pictures of farm scenes, homes, and bright clouds. I liked those quaint photographs; they symbolized God's tender care. In particular the clouds connected me to my Grandma Crawford's farm. We drove to see Grandma on Sunday afternoons—sunny days filled with white cumulus clouds in the sky. As we passed the local scenery, downtown sat silent, and the countryside was beautiful. As little kid, who missed the significance of symbolism, I thought, *God and the heavenly host live in the clouds, and here, above our town and countryside, are clouds. Where else can heaven be but here, directly above our town? Why else would clouds fill the covers of our Sunday school magazine—clouds that looked the same as these clouds outside, creating shapes that God decreed, and overlooking countrysides like this?* A feeling of peace pervaded our small town space, and with it came a depth that seemed to promise a greater peace.

These thoughts are, of course, interpretations of feelings recollected many years later after I left for college and astonished everyone, including myself, with an interest in deepening my spiritual life and eventually following a religious career. But in reality, my life path wasn't so astounding. Without realizing, I was touched profoundly by a *place*, and the beginning of my spiritual journey was no more ostentatious than a pleasant sojourn in the nooks and rooms of a small church. *Place*, to paraphrase Jesus, was the storehouse of treasures old and new.

god's wide places

Have you ever known a place (either indoors or outdoors) where you felt moved, unexpectedly inspired, or profoundly comforted? Has a special place given you exactly the perspective you needed? Have you reacted spiritually (whether in a religious or nonreligious way) to a particular location? Have you ever looked back on your life and believed that God had guided you as you went about your life in a certain place? Does a place in your current life help you "connect" with God?

The topics of "the sense of place" and "sacred space" have earned attention in several books in recent years.[1] In this book I'll explore ways God meets us in the places of our lives—guiding, alerting, inspiring, convicting, and providing insight, comfort, and understanding. I'll consider place as one of the "things" in the statement, "all things work together for good for those who love God, who are called according to his purpose" (Rom. 8:28). I'll also look at places that are "spiritual" in a broad sense. My approach is informal and invitational.

Making no effort to be comprehensive, I reflect on notable locations in my own journey and share special places contributed by several of my friends. In doing so I offer you the chance to think about places special to you, to reflect on how God moves in your life.

We'll also traverse the Bible to discover places where God touched people with divine grace. Rather than examine the important, "big" sacred places like the Temple, the Tabernacle, and the "holy sites" of Jesus' life, I focus on some of the Bible's more everyday locations: a well, a tree, a road, a field, a rock, and so on. Critical as it is for biblical faith, I only consider the Promised Land itself briefly.[2] Trips to "holy places" can be tremendously meaningful, but most of us are more likely to know God among the everyday, inauspicious locations. Yet we might tempted to downplay everyday places, seeking "big" signs of grace.

My title comes from Psalm 18:36: "You gave me a wide place for my steps under me, and my feet did not slip." The psalmist looked at circumstances and felt threatened by difficulties and dangers, as if traveling upon a narrow, rocky height without safety and sure footing. Picture yourself hiking in a rocky area or even driving the switchbacks of a two-lane mountain highway; the psalmist has chosen an apt analogy for life's hazards! Yet God's care went with him.

We find this image of "the wide place" elsewhere. Note these lines from other psalms:

> Answer me when I call, O God of my right!
> You gave me room when I was in distress.
> Be gracious to me, and hear my prayer. (Psalm 4:1)

There is a contrast in the original language. The Hebrew word *rahab*, used in the phrase "you gave me room," also means "wide" while the word *sar*, "distress," also means "narrow."[3] Other psalms contain similar language.

> He brought me out into a broad place;
> he delivered me, because he delighted in me. (Psalm 18:19)

> [You] have not delivered me into the hand of the enemy;
> you have set my feet in a broad place. (Psalm 31:8)
>
> Out of my distress I called on the LORD;
> the LORD answered me and set me in a broad place. (Psalm 118:5)

The psalms also give us lovely, spatial images of "dwelling" in God's grace. "In peace I will both lie down and sleep; for thou alone, O LORD, makest me dwell in safety" (Ps. 4:8, RSV). Perhaps the most famous psalm of all, Psalm 23, is filled with "place" images of well-being: green pastures and still waters, a table set by a generous host, and a dwelling place in the house of the Lord. Even the difficult place of the psalm, "the darkest valley," holds no dread for the poet, because God provides all that humans need.

The psalmists speak poetically, but the image of the wide place is filled with implications: God not only gives us grace and divine presence but actively creates "space" in our places and circumstances. Thus one of my main goals in this book is to help us identify those divine wide places in the locations sacred to us: a room, a historical site, a natural wonder, a highway, a church, or a childhood spot.

Places can also be dark, fearsome valleys, and I want to examine a few of those. Sometimes we don't connect such places with God's care until we regard them in hindsight, especially when God gently leads us with a still, small voice. (The well-known story "Footprints in the Sand" comes to mind; the punch line is that the narrator has been unaware, even doubtful, of God's help during difficult times.) Other locations become significant milestones of grace to which we return, at least in memory, again and again. Psalm 18:36 speaks not only to particular wide places but also to the wideness of God's mercy, which covers the range of human experience.

the grace of the ordinary

I use the phrase "wide place" more often than the venerable "holy ground." Holy ground also refers to places where God touches our lives in significant ways. Other metaphors serve well to describe God's presence, including *shekinah*, a term with a long and hallowed tradition in Judaism, and "thin places" that originates in Celtic Christianity. *Shekinah* (or *shechinah*) is the glory or emanation of God manifested in the Tabernacle, and also in human acts of righteousness and compassion.[4] Thin places are locations and experiences—and also people and religious practices—where God's presence is felt strongly.[5]

When I told one friend about this project, she humorously called herself "feng shui deficient." She referred to the Chinese philosophy of harmonious arrangement of objects and colors and the beneficial placement of one's home within a proper landscape. But she meant that she had no places in her life more special than others. You may feel the same way, or perhaps your special places seem very ordinary.

Yet it was an ordinary location where Jacob declared, "Surely the LORD is in this place—and I did not know it!" (Gen. 28:16). As my friend Tom H. puts it, "For God, miracles are an easy way of getting our attention. The ordinary requires God to take a chance." Let us look at places that God touched, and touches still!

about the exercises

You can use this book either for individual reflection or in a small-group setting. Every chapter ends with five exercises, each lasting about ten minutes. Use these exercises as you like: pick and choose, modify, or add to them according to your needs. Don't beat yourself up if you don't do all five. Enjoy deepening your spiritual life! Discover what is true for your life and spiritual journey.

In the Small-Group Guide you'll find prayers and discussion/study questions you can use separately or in conjunction with the exercises.

1 the lord is a place

What are your favorite places? A busy street in an urban downtown? A mountain in a rugged landscape? An amazing vista such as Niagara Falls? A temple in Greece? A cathedral in Europe? An old tree beside the highway? Perhaps you love a room or chair in your house, or an area in the woods, or by a stream or lake.

Perhaps your favorite place is no longer part of your life. It was your grandmother's house, or your childhood home, or a country to which you haven't returned. For instance, I love Israel/Palestine, but I've only been there once. Perhaps your favorite place is a childhood park, or an undeveloped location (a creek or woods) that you explored as a child. Or maybe your favorite place is a location you visit comparatively seldom, like a vacation spot.

If I let my mind wander, I think of other places I love: the wonderful people and landscapes of Pope County, Illinois, where I served three small churches in the 1980s; the sidewalks of downtown

Chicago, where my family and I shopped; the campus of Yale Divinity School; the farms along Interstate 64 in southern Indiana; the Cloisters in New York; the small towns of Waldo and Obetz, Ohio, where my ancestors are buried.

Important places certainly can be ordinary or extraordinary. I'll always remember the first time I saw newly fallen snow on the San Francisco Peaks as I drove along old Route 66 in Flagstaff, Arizona, our home for four years; the autumn color of the Shenandoah Valley in Virginia; the hilly vistas of New England. I fondly remember a grocery store where I ran errands, a roadside picnic table along a beloved, rural highway, and many other places.

Some locations resonate negatively. Many of us struggled socially through middle school or high school and don't care to relive such memories by returning to our old schools. Nor do we want to linger mentally or literally at an unhappy place of employment or a place where we faced danger, such as a crime scene or combat zone. Even a favorite place can be painful. My wife, Beth, has little desire to revisit the site of her grandparents' farm near Cleveland, Tennessee. She spent many happy days there, but now the buildings are gone and nothing is the same.

The Greek word *topos*, from which we derive such English words as *utopia* and *topographical*, can mean "place" or "space." Several years ago a writer coined the term *topophilia*, "the love of place," to describe the multifaceted human attachment to environment.[1] You could say that "place" is any physical space that, for whatever reason, is important and meaningful. Place is space that is both remembered and evocative of memories.[2] Place is space with a history.[3]

what makes a place?

Many factors combine to make a place significant. First is the setting. What is the place's geographical and social nature? Is it urban or rural? What is it like geographically and naturally?

Of course, some settings command our attention, fill us with wonder, and humble us—think of natural wonders, architectural marvels, tremendous cities, ancient sites. Other places are not extraordinary but no less dear. A particular street, an old tree, a fencerow, a shoreline: these things stir you at a more personal, subjective level.

Why do such places carry deep connections for you? Because your personal history makes a place special. Your experiences, tastes, and attitudes combine to form your response to that place. What in your personal history makes a place agreeable or disagreeable? Why is that hill or canyon or street dear to your heart—or a place you avoid?

When you live in a community, your personal history defines your response to it. Are you living in this place or just visiting? Is the community a comfortable size? Have you had success or failure here? Pleasant or disagreeable experiences? If you've been here a while, what milestone events occurred here?

Other people also affect our response to place. Who are your neighbors and associates? Who makes the place lovely—or unpleasant? Do you click with people? When you have a need, do people respond or not? Feeling helpless and alone in a community, even temporarily, can sour you forever on that location, regardless of its benefits.

Sometimes we enjoy a place at a specific time in our life, but we wouldn't later. The time of your life also holds significance. A place can "happen" to us at the right time or the wrong time. I lived in an eastern state as a graduate student. My time in that place was defined, in large measure, by the stresses and indignities of being a student. So I never enjoyed the area as much as I might have had I lived there in other circumstances.

Places also become important because they give you a new perspective. Places challenge you and make you realize your life may be too busy, off track, or out of focus. My friend Stacey, a nurse and ice skating instructor in northeast Ohio, writes:

> Perhaps the most spiritual and relaxing place I have ever seen was the Rocky Mountains. However, it was not the industrialized portion of the mountains, not the place with all of the shopping plazas and ski resorts (although I enjoyed that too). No, it was reaching the top of one the many peaks and resting as fresh snow fell. I felt completely alone and at peace. You realize how small and insignificant the ordeals of everyday life are as you sit atop one of the largest mountains in the country. There really is another world out there, a world not many of us realize exists until we stop the hustle and bustle of insignificant everyday ordeals.

An easily overlooked aspect of our response to place is the larger history. Does this place have qualities of which you're unaware or take for granted? What is the settlement history of the area? Do past situations (conflicts between whites and Native Americans, or the presence of slavery, and so on) provide a mixed heritage for that region? Has your property been developed from natural regions? I loved our house and neighborhood in Flagstaff. It was the house to which we brought our infant daughter from the hospital. But our garage door repairman lamented the neighborhood. He missed the days when that same land was undeveloped and comparatively pristine.

We can simplify these ideas by saying that our places and stories are inseparably linked. By "stories" I simply mean the aspects of life that are most important to our sense of identity. A place resonates with you because it is part of your story. A place is wonderful because it is a deep part of your story—maybe that place is a "character" therein! Or a place is terrible because it's connected to a hard time or painful event in your story.

Places are clearly inexhaustible in meaning because the very idea of place is defined by both the physical space and the human response. A church, for instance, can be warm and welcoming to one person but cold and restrictive to another. A tree I remember, once my favorite climbing tree, has no special meaning to you.

The more public and symbolic a place—tied to national and international meanings—the deeper and more varied is its significance. Think of the Vietnam Memorial in Washington, D.C. That monument evokes as many reactions as there are visitors. Think of the Gettysburg battlefield; many people find it moving, while others feel distracted by its many plaques and monuments. Places open up possibilities of conflict, debate, and interpretation, especially places embraced by many people. The city of Jerusalem and other Holy Land sites are revered by persons of three different faiths, but the meaning of these sites is disputed even among people of the same faith.[4]

what makes a place sacred?

As I think about special places, I'm apt to describe some as sacred. We might say that a place is sacred to us simply because it is extremely special; it has no formal religious connotation but we identify strongly with that location. We don't want anything bad to happen to it. We'd lose a part of ourselves if it ceased to be. A certain prairie in Illinois, about which I'll write later, is such a place for me.

A place can be sacred because something significant happened there. Many visitors consider sacred the house in Akron, Ohio, where two men founded Alcoholics Anonymous in 1935. One of my own sacred places is the state capitol in my hometown. Lincoln began his political career in the legislature there, so the place is not only a Lincoln shrine but also sacred to local heritage. Lincoln's legal and political experiences in Vandalia prepared him for the presidency.

A battlefield and the site of a tragedy are properly called sacred places because human lives were lost there. Recall Lincoln's well-known remarks at Gettysburg: the honored dead hallowed that place with their sacrifice. Similarly the 9/11/01 sites: the World Trade Center, the Pentagon, and the Pennsylvania crash site. As author Frank McCourt puts it, "There has never been shrine-making as there was after September 11. . . . Manhattan had become sacred."[5]

War memorials certainly are sacred places because they honor the memory of the dead.

Very ordinary places can become personal sanctuaries in terrible times. Julie, a college professor on the East Coast, writes:

> There is a tiny patch of wilderness near our home, where we often hike. But once, around September 13 or 14, 2001, after we had driven to New York to pick up my stepdaughter, Miriam, whose high school, a few blocks from the former World Trade Center, was closed, we took her there. Miriam, along with our son, Aaron, swung on vines and dog-paddled around in the stream, and felt all the healing of a small piece of nature after the horrors she had watched a few days before. Before that day, I loved the park. Since that day it is sacred.

Places of religious pilgrimage are sacred too. Think of the Hindu faith; for some Hindus, visits to shrines are a crucial aspect of worship.[6] Think of the holy Kaaba in the Muslim faith; Muslims certainly don't believe God is localized there, but the pilgrimage to Mecca is an important expression of their faith. In the Christian Middle Ages certain places were important sites for pilgrimages too. God is, of course, everywhere, so making pilgrimage is an optional kind of worship, though important to many.[7] Jews look to the Promised Land as a place where the Lord has worked in their history and destiny with mighty acts still remembered and honored.

These are "big" locations that, in different ways, anchor religious faith. More personally, we could also say a place is sacred because God came to us at that location: we had some kind of experience or insight or sense of peace at that place, which by faith we attribute to God's presence. Or we associate that location with someone who was extremely influential to us. In memory, if not physically, we return to that spot and are reassured.

The other general meanings of "sacred" can certainly overlap with a sense of God's presence. In fact, the heightened sense of emotion we experience in sacred places may be a gift from God or a way by which we're moved to seek God. If we argue about the specifics of the place—in what sense is it sacred and why—we might miss the grace, which is God's initiative, not ours.

god is our place

What is the relationship of God and the places of our lives? We could end this book right now by simply affirming God's ubiquity; God is everywhere, at all times. Consider Psalm 139:7-10:

> Where can I go from your spirit?
> Or where can I flee from your presence?
> If I ascend to heaven, you are there;
> if I make my bed in Sheol, you are there.
> If I take the wings of the morning
> and settle at the farthest limits of the sea,
> even there your hand shall lead me,
> and your right hand shall hold me fast.

If I want to find a place to avoid God, just for a short time for myself in my own personal space, I fail—because God is there too.

When we read the Old Testament in close detail, we discover passages where God seems to be localized: Moses encounter with God on the mountain in Exodus 19; Elijah's experience of God in 1 Kings 19; the presence of God in the Temple. God even calls the people to meet God for worship at a certain place of God's choosing (Deut. 16:16), and later declares that Mount Zion is God's dwelling place (Isa. 8:18). And yet, in these passages, God's locality is a special presence rather than a static source of power available only at that place.[8] Even the Temple was not intended as the only place God lived, as the prophets stressed (e.g., Jer. 7:1-7; 22:16; and also Isaiah 66:1-2, quoted again in Acts 7:48-50).

God is sometimes called "place," but as a metaphor for the divine continual presence wherever we seek it. God is our *machseh*, a word translated as "dwelling place" (Deut. 33:27, RSV) or "refuge" (KJV and NIV). Psalm 46:1 declares that "God is our refuge and strength, a very present help in trouble." Another Hebrew word, *m'ownah*, is frequently used in the Bible to refer to particular locations—notably in Genesis 28:17, where Jacob declares, "How awesome is this place!" But rabbis after the biblical period adopted this word as a metaphorical name for God. The Jewish philosopher Philo wrote, "God . . . is called place, for He encompasses all things, but is not encompassed by anything."[9] To call God "place" means not only that God is omnipresent but also (in the words of a Jewish midrash) is "the place of the world."[10]

As Abraham Millgram puts it, "The religious Jew worshiped God everywhere and at all times. Every experience was an occasion for a benediction, every place was sanctified by God's presence, and every moment was permeated with divine grace."[11] The Talmud has a wonderful story about a Jewish boy aboard a ship caught in a storm. While the Gentiles prayed to idols, the boy prayed to the Lord. Later the sailors said to him, "We are here, but our gods are in Babylon or Rome; and others amongst us who carry their gods with them derive not the least benefit from them. But you, wherever you go, your God is with you."[12]

Christians, like Jews, honored God as unbounded by time and space, the God who is a dwelling and refuge for all who call upon God. Jesus becomes the "place to go" to know God in spirit and truth (Matt. 7:24-25; John 4:21-24), the "new thing" God has done by which we might know God (Isa. 43:19; Heb. 1:1-2). Jesus is the place that encompasses all places, because in and through him all things came to be (Col. 1:15-20). Not only that, but through Jesus Christ God has broken down all barriers and accomplished all that is necessary for peace, reconciliation, and salvation (Eph. 1:5-14; 2:8-14). God is present for us in whatever place we are, until the close of time (Matt. 28:20; Rev. 22:13).

where did god go?

So there is no question about God's presence—or is there? Think of Psalm 42:1-3:

> As a deer longs for flowing streams,
> so my soul longs for you, O God.
> My soul thirsts for God,
> for the living God.
> When shall I come and behold the face of God?
> My tears have been my food
> day and night,
> while people say to me continually,
> "Where is your God?"

The psalmist is troubled, but God's ubiquity is not the issue. Nor is the psalmist fleeing God. The psalmist is fleeing *to* God, but God seems missing. Psalms 42 and 43, lament psalms, actually belong together. The psalmist uses another metaphor for God that connotes a permanent place: "I say to God, my rock, 'Why have you forgotten me?'" (42:9). "Rock" (in Hebrew, *sela*) is another frequent image for God. God is aptly named "rock" because rocks (large ones, anyway) are reliably in place, and large rocky formations are both symbols of strength and points for navigation.

The psalmist lived away from Jerusalem (42:6) and, perhaps because of illness (42:10), could not attend the Temple ceremonies—happy times he poignantly remembers (42:4). A dear lady in my first parish stayed at home most of the time; she was elderly, and her husband required care. She told me how much she missed going to church! She knew that she could pray at home, and she did. But she regretted the loss of her congregation—her special place.

The psalmist would praise God (42:5-6, 11; 43:5) but not at this particular stage. Here, in God's own Word, is a song about a person who can't find God.

If God is omnipresent and eager to be our rock and refuge, why do we have to search for God?

chapter 1

where are you?

For many of us, spirituality is a key part of our stories. Spirituality can be a rich, exciting thing of discovery and insight—part of the "religious adventure" of life.[13] In his book *Landscapes of the Soul: A Spirituality of Place*, Robert M. Hamma points out that spirituality can be called a recognition of a three-part relationship: with God, others, and ourselves.[14] Our spirituality is healthiest when we hold these dimensions together.

Spirituality is not necessarily a comfort zone. Most of us, myself included, prefer a spiritual path that builds inner peace, self-esteem, confidence in times of trouble, and so on. We prefer not to embark upon a spiritual path that leads to painful inner change and difficult questions! Rabbi Niles Elliot Goldstein writes in *God at the Edge* that "Much of what passes for spirituality these days is approached from a perspective that is comforting and clean." Many spiritual paths, he says, focus upon "the serenity, sensitivity, and self-love that are often beyond our grasp."[15] The spiritual path certainly leads to positive outcomes, but it can also lead us out of our familiar routine and demand significant changes in our thinking and patterns of living.

Although we speak of searching for God, God is actually the one who takes the initiative in the search! The very first question asked in the Bible is God's question to Adam and Eve at the place Eden.

> They heard the sound of the LORD God walking in the garden at the time of the evening breeze, and the man and his wife hid themselves from the presence of the LORD God among the trees of the garden. But the LORD God called to the man, and said to him, "Where are you?" (Genesis 3:8-9)

This wonderful story portrays God with a lovely innocence. We can explain God's question theologically: since God is omnipotent, the question rhetorically confronts Adam and Eve. But for now let us simply appreciate the story as it is: God enjoyed the beautiful place and called to Adam and Eve because God temporarily lost track of them. But Adam and Eve were hiding from God. Did God experience foreboding? Sure enough, they had done the single thing that God had forbidden. This couple consequently felt self-conscious, ashamed, and unsure what to do next.

Adam and Eve forthrightly told God what they'd done, although they immediately played the blame game (vv. 12-13). The couple had not maliciously rebelled against God. They ate the fruit out of a kind of thickheaded, childish confusion about God's original instructions. The story is like a comedy where a child might hide in the cupboard and talk to Mom or Dad through the door, explaining what happened to the cookies in the cookie jar. But the Garden is no comedy.

We all hide from God at one time or another. Although David went about his daily routine, perhaps even satisfied with the outcome of his deed, he nevertheless hid from God following his marriage to Bathsheba. By the time Nathan confronted him, David had, on one level at least, put the whole matter behind him. When we hide in similar fashion, God sees us; but we disregard God, hoping God will put us out of mind and move on to more willing subjects!

We all hide from God at one time or another.

Sometimes when God asks us, "Where are you?" our response is, "I'm not completely sure. Psychologically as well as spiritually I'm disconnected from God. My life is filled—too full, in fact—with activities, even very positive activities. I'm too tired or too busy to feel prayerful or sensitive to God's guidance."

Sometimes we drift from God, to use an image from the book of Hebrews (2:1). You may know the feeling: your faith was once strong, but thanks to a variety of circumstances, you've changed and don't really believe anymore. You're not even sure God exists. Yet being spiritually empty may be a sign of God's grace!

Perhaps something happened that made you question God. A life crisis tested your faith; you're struggling with grief, or memories of abuse or violence, and healing is difficult. The crisis might even have been a church controversy of some sort; you feel deeply betrayed by "good religious people." Or perhaps you simply have honest questions about God. You're skeptical about institutions. The usual theological answers don't satisfy you; you're unsure that you or anyone else can make a difference in the world. But you're a "believing nonbeliever,"[16] still open to grace.

Perhaps you feel that your spiritual life is moving in a good direction, with normal full and dry periods. But you're restless until your understanding of God grows stronger. You could not do without your relationship with God, but you know you lack in understanding, and in some key ways your relationship is deficient.

Perhaps you think you're spiritually full, but you're really quite empty. This may be the most risky spiritual place of all. Becoming self-possessed in faith, focused on the proverbial to-do lists that you (not God) create in your religious life, is hazardous. "Knowledge puffs up, but love builds up," writes Paul. "Anyone who claims to know something does not yet have the necessary knowledge; but anyone who loves God is known by him" (1 Cor. 8:1-3). Paul writes to Christians who had the right doctrine but considered themselves spiritually superior to other Christians. People typically think of "falling from grace" as the result of moral failure, but Paul cautions the Galatians that falling from grace actually happens through an excess of religion (Gal. 5:4).

All of these are "places" on the spiritual journey, and God's grace is present in all these places! God gives us faith and encourages even the smallest flicker that may remain (Isa. 42:3).

spirituality and place

If you do a free association on the word *spirituality*, "place" may not be among the first words to pop into your mind. Perhaps you think of prayer, public worship, solitary time, reading, doing selfless things, working for justice, and so on. Yet language about spirituality is filled with images of place. I've already used the phrases "spiritual path" and "comfort zone," which connote places of travel and safety. We speak of faith as if it were a highway from place to place: we're "on the way," we're on a "faith journey," and when we get lost we need "direction." We also speak of "returning," as in repentance. (One of James W. Moore's books on Christian faith is *If You're Going the Wrong Way . . . Turn Around!*[17]) We talk about our spiritual "homes," the many rooms in our Father's house (John 14), even of "shopping around," not in a favorite business district or mall but in search of a congregation in which to serve and worship.

It is comforting to express our faith in terms of physical space, not only because we're imperfect (we haven't reached our destination) but because places fill our days.

Places are also integral parts of our spirituality in so far as we grow in God's grace among the locations of our lives. As Robert Hamma puts it, "Particular places provide a structure and a context for our spirituality. . . . Christians, and indeed all religious people, have always had a sense of the importance of sacred places. . . . What is new today is a growing awareness of how our experience of places and spaces shapes our spirituality. . . . An increasing number of people are paying attention to how the ordinary places of their lives affect their awareness of God, of themselves, and of others. The 'who,' the 'how,' and the 'when' of our spiritual lives derive their distinctiveness in large measure from the 'where.'"[18]

By reflecting on our spiritual geographies,[19] we make several interrelated discoveries. We understand God's work in our lives more clearly; we understand ourselves more clearly. We appreciate why particular places have been wonderful or painful for us. We clarify our place on our spiritual journeys; we grow in faith. By growing in faith, we draw closer to God; we change for the better (hopefully, ideally); and we find new ways to serve others.

Let us recall three well-known stories from the Bible in which God becomes known in ordinary places: a stone, a bush, and a road.

for i will not leave you

Jacob is one of those Bible characters I associate with my childhood church. In vacation Bible school children's literature, Jacob was a small cartoon man dressed in robe and sandals, standing beside his much-larger brother, Esau—like Popeye and Bluto, only Jacob advanced because of trickery rather than spinach. As I walked the small-town sidewalks back home, that dreamy, melancholy song "Jacob's Ladder" stuck in my mind: "Sinner . . . do you . . . love my . . . Jesus? . . . Soldiers . . . of the . . . cross."

Jacob's story seems bleaker now, a saga of betrayal and revenge. We know the story: how Rebekah and Jacob deceived Isaac so Jacob could receive the elder son's blessing (Gen. 27:5-29). Why was so much at stake? What was the power of a spoken blessing or a spoken curse? If I told you, in all seriousness, "You're really ugly," or "You'll never amount to anything," and if my opinion mattered to you, you would understand the power of words! And that's just the psychological effect of words—strong enough to change lives. In biblical times, a blessing or curse could make the words actually *happen* beyond the psychological effect (v. 33).

After he deceived his father, Jacob fled his home place to stay with Rebekah's brother, Laban (Gen. 27:43–28:5), although the text gives two different reasons for Jacob's hiding. He left Beer-sheba and traveled toward Haran, where Laban livedd. Haran lay far to the north and east from Canaan in the area of the upper Euphrates. Jacob hadd not yet left Canaan when he came to a certain, inauspicious place. The sun had set, so he stopped, settled in, and rested his head upon a stone (Gen. 28:11).

Falling asleep at that place, he dreamed of a stairway (or ladder or ramp; the text can be translated differently), with angels ascending and descending between earth and heaven:

> And the LORD stood beside him and said, "I am the LORD, the God of Abraham your father and the God of Isaac; the land on which you lie I will give to you and to your offspring; and your offspring shall be like the dust of the earth, and you shall spread abroad to the west and to the east and to the north and to the south; and all the families of the earth shall be blessed in you and in your offspring. Know that I am with you and will keep you wherever you go, and will bring you back to this land; for I will not leave you until I have done what I have promised you." (Genesis 28:13-15)

Jacob awoke and exclaimed, "Surely the LORD is in this place—and I did not know it!" He added, "How awesome is this place! This is none other than the house of God, and this is the gate of heaven" (vv. 16-17).

"Awesome!" is a common exclamatory phrase these days, similar to the impossibly dated "Groovy!" But the Hebrew word can also be translated "dreadful," in the sense of "full of dread and awe." Perhaps Jacob was filled with anxiety and uncertainty rather than happy astonishment.

Somehow Jacob went back to sleep; but when he arose, he took the stone on which he had slept, stood it up as a pillar, and anointed it with oil. He established the stone as a recognizable, sacred place and called it Bethel—which means House of God—and made a vow to the Lord: "If God will be with me, and will keep me in this way that I go, and will give me bread to eat and clothing to wear, so that I come again to my father's house in peace, then the LORD shall be my God, and this stone, which I have set up for a pillar, shall be God's house; and of all that you give me I will surely give one-tenth to you" (vv. 20-22).

Jewish commentators note that this is an immature but honest prayer from the heart.[20] Years ago I heard a church speaker recounting the times when he argued with God. One day he wanted a sign from God and asked God to show him a four-leaf clover in his yard. The man had never been able to find a four-leaf clover, ever. This time he found several. Whether we're far along the way of faith or at the beginning of our spiritual journey, our faith may be at a place where we need help from God.

Jacob's adventures were only the beginning. He traveled to Haran, met Laban and his family, and was deceived into long service to his uncle (Gen. 29:1–31:55). What did he think about during his years of labor? Did he miss his home? His parents? Did he dread the time he would someday confront his brother, Esau? Did he ruminate upon his strange encounter with God?

The place called Bethel was holy because God came to it. The place became for Jacob a memory and reminder of God's faithfulness. What is your Bethel?

holy ground

A few years ago, I listened as a church choir sang the hymn "We Are Standing in His Presence on Holy Ground." I wondered how true that was. There we sat quietly, worshipers in our Sunday clothes, some of us (like me) caffeinated and a little sleepy. My family and I sat in the same pew as always. This is holy ground?

I'm not implying that the singers were insincere in their performance or that we worshipers were hypocrites. But I thought of Annie Dillard's comment in *Teaching a Stone to Talk*. "Why do we people in churches seem like cheerful, brainless tourists on a packaged tour of the Absolute? . . . Does anyone have the foggiest idea what sort of power we so blithely invoke? Or, as I suspect, does no one believe a word of it?"[21]

That overstates it—or perhaps not. What do we expect in our spirituality? God loves us and comforts us. But God also challenges and directs us. God changes us, if we allow it; and change is never easy. When Moses stood on holy ground, the experience was frightening and life changing.

In an important story of Hebrew scriptures, Moses was working—

tending his father-in-law's flock of sheep in the wilderness at Mount Horeb (also known as Sinai). We could speculate (although the text does not say so) that Moses had been by this place before or at least the area was familiar.

Some time—a long time, in fact (Exod. 2:23)—had passed since Moses' youth and his flight from Egypt after killing the Egyptian tormentor (Exod. 2:11-15). We imagine how he remembered his earlier life: as a still-sharp memory, as a chapter in his life now dulled to memory, or as a time that returned to mind occasionally, only to retreat to more comfortable mental places.

As Moses tended the sheep, an angel appeared to him in a bush that burned but was not consumed. Scripture tells us nothing specific about this place. In my mind I picture the bush and its location as a lovely place at the foot of the mountain, one of those nooks that nature sometimes provides. But perhaps the place looked as common as the little grassy places beside stores where we shop, the patch of wildflowers and bramble at the back of my yard, the neglected areas we glimpse as we pass by, traveling elsewhere. The biblical text focuses on the appearance of God in a noticeable form: no earthquake or lightning but an incredible, small sight. Perhaps Moses heard it before he saw it: a gentle crackle of flame some place off to the side of his daily chores.

Moses took the time to look. Because he did, God called to him (Exod. 3:4). He responded, "Here I am!" (*Hinneni*), the same attentive way Abraham responded to God (Gen. 22:1).

God commanded Moses to remove his sandals, "for the place on which you are standing is holy ground" (Exod. 3:5). Going barefoot into religious sanctuaries is a common practice in several faiths. I remember removing my shoes when visiting the Dome of the Rock in Jerusalem and when visiting a Sikh assembly (*gurdwara*) in Ohio. The idea is to enter the facility clean—without your dusty old shoes on—and humble—without shoes; rich and poor alike come before God at the same social level. Also, as one Jewish commentator puts it, "Only when one is barefoot can one feel the little stones underfoot. Moses was to lead his people in such a way that he could feel their smallest sorrows."[22]

> God said to Moses, "I AM WHO I AM." He said further, "Thus you shall say to the Israelites, 'I AM has sent me to you.'" God also said to Moses, "Thus you shall say to the Israelites, 'The LORD, the God of your ancestors, the God of Abraham, the God of Isaac, and the God of Jacob, has sent me to you':
> This is my name forever,
> and this is my title for all generations."
> (Exodus 3:14-15)

God heard the cries of the Hebrews, enslaved in Egypt, and had a plan to free them. God chose Moses as leader.

Notice how Moses responded. Humbled at this holy place, he was respectful but did not grovel. He even argued with God: "If the Israelites ask who sent me, what should I tell them? What if they say, 'Moses, you dreamed the whole thing'?" He argued further: "Why me, God? I'm not a good speaker." None of these questions "worked." Finally, Moses said, "O my Lord, please send someone else" (Exod. 4:13).

At that point "the anger of the LORD was kindled against Moses" (v. 14). But I linger on Moses' dignity, his questioning. Faith is not an unquestioning suppression of our humanness. Nor is faith a smiling acceptance of a strange turn of events when inside we feel pain and doubt.

As Moses went about his everyday life, God spoke to him in a common place, in a way noticeable but not ostentatious. The place became an occasion to meet God, to receive a call, to move in the direction of faith—and to grapple with God, which is also part of faith. Holy ground was, for Moses, the beginning of a lifelong, eventful friendship with God—and the blessing of an entire people. What is your holy ground?

on the road

When I recall Bible passages where God appeared to people at a certain place, I also turn to the familiar story in Luke 24 of the road to Emmaus.

My father was a truck driver who hauled gasoline to stations around southern and south-central Illinois, so my love of highways comes naturally. Highway signs and trademark symbols fill me with a strange homesickness, whether for home or the road, I'm not always sure. If I could, I'd show you many rural, roadside locations of no significance other than my own nostalgia. I even teach a course called American Highways and American Wanderlust at the University of Akron.

My car has become my sanctum sanctorum.

I often drive or walk whenever I need a change of pace. On the road I feel a sense of peace and perspective. Walking is better, because I'm not separated from the landscape. But driving is also a joy. My friend Tom D. is a talented poet who leads a busy life, but that doesn't stop him from letting the natural world speak to him spiritually.

> Although I've been blessed with many holy places, right now my holiest place may well be my car. I drive to and from work almost every day through the Cuyahoga Valley National Park. My car has become my sanctum sanctorum, and the view, internally and externally, changes every day. I bring my griefs and joys to the deer in the cornfields, the raccoons, the ever-changing trees, the covered bridge, the runners and bikers. Sometimes I play bluegrass gospel or Leontyne Price's gospel and spirituals CDs; sometimes I sing myself; sometimes I just pray. Often I slow down or pull over so those who think life goes to the swiftest can pass. No matter how busy I am, the park comforts my soul. The great thing about my car, of course, is that I can take it to a lot of places; they too become my holy places.

Evening walks gave me comfort during a time when I felt particularly lonely and distressed. About that same time I discovered Robert Frost's poem "Acquainted with the Night."[23] In that sonnet, the poet takes long walks in the nightime, even in rain. He feels isolated and downcast, but what troubles him? Perhaps the poet wanted to escape a situation or to gain perspective. His walks seem to solve no problems, whatever they may be, although the image of the clock implies acceptance of the circumstance. One also thinks of Isaiah 53:3 and Jesus' "acquaintance" with grief. Frost's poem is suitably ambiguous. As with his more famous poem "Stopping by Woods on a Snowy Evening," we feel the emotions without needing to understand biographical details. What do you think about whenyou take walks?

The reason the two disciples traveled to Emmaus is similarly ambiguous. Perhaps they needed to remove themselves from the events at Jerusalem: Jesus was dead and buried. What more could they do? Frederick Buechner likens Emmaus to any place we go when life no longer makes sense and we need to escape.[24] Prior to Jesus' arrival, the walk to Emmaus was one of temporary peace but no lasting consolation.

The two men, one named Cleopas and the other unnamed, walked into the sunset—a stereotypical time for stories to conclude. My pastor friend Jim says, "Sometimes God is like a preacher. Have you ever heard a preacher who missed one, two, or sometimes three or more great opportunities to end the sermon? God is like that at Easter."

Just as you think the story is ending, a man appears to Cleopas and his friend. Of course, they do not recognize the man. The newcomer is strange because he's unfamiliar and, apparently, clueless. "What are you discussing with each other while you walk along?" he asked. Cleopas answered him with a retort like, "What planet have you been on the last few days?" He explained to the stranger about Jesus—and not only Jesus but the dashed dreams and confusion that accompanied Jesus' violent end (Luke 24:19-24). The stranger, Jesus, replied, seemingly harshly, "Was it not necessary that the Messiah should suffer these things and then enter into his glory?" (v. 26). As they walked along, Jesus interpreted the scriptures to the two downcast men.

People who do all the talking can be vexatious or fascinating. Jesus was fascinating—so much so that the two men felt alarmed when the stranger indicated that Emmaus was not his ultimate destination. "Stay with us!" they declared. Later, when Jesus blessed the bread, broke it, and gave it to them, the two men realized who Jesus was. But he vanished.

"Were not our hearts burning within us while he was talking to us on the road, while he was opening the scriptures to us?" one of the men asked rhetorically (v. 32). God appeared to them, not in a burning bush this time but in their burning hearts—more precisely, in the words of Jesus and the sharing of the bread. Even though it was late in the day (and they'd already walked approximately seven miles to Emmaus), the men went back to Jerusalem and found Jesus' other disciples to tell them what had happened.

My friend Pastor Jim continues, "Throughout history Jesus consistently shows up in the lives of people who have called his name. Sometimes Jesus even shows up in the lives of those who do not call his name." In what places in your life has Jesus "showed up" in a strong and clear way? Are there places where, like the two friends going to Emmaus, you were touched by God's presence and you only understood in retrospect?

As we traverse several different kinds of places and several more scriptures, we can assess our own journeys and see how places of our lives served to draw us closer to God.

exercises

1. In a notebook, list five favorite places. Rank them 1 through 5. Write down why each is special to you.

2. List your five most sacred places and rank them 1 through 5. (They could overlap with the first five.) Recall the different kinds of sacredness discussed in chapter 1 and write down why these places are sacred and in what sense.

3. List your least favorite places. Describe them briefly: what happened there, what spoiled the place, and so on. Do you nevertheless associate any with the presence of God? Are there any redeeming qualities to those places?

4. Imagine being on a journey, perhaps walking a path or driving a road. Then visualize Christ accompanying you. What does he say to you? What directions does he give?

5. Physically place yourself in a peaceful location. Perhaps it's the spot where you usually read and pray or perhaps an outdoor location (if weather permits). Reflect on your present relationship with God—the "place" on your spiritual journey. Are you close to God? Are you drifting away? Do you feel cynical? Are you not sure? Imagine God asking you, in a loving and interested way, "Where are you?" How do you answer? Do you feel happy, angry, or embarrassed when God asks?

2 home places

I'm writing this chapter on a computer that sits atop our kitchen island. Our living room and kitchen are continuous, so I can write with classical music playing on the living room stereo. Then when it's time to cook, I'm only a few steps away. When I need a snack, the pantry is right behind me. I tell myself that the intense mental effort of writing a book demands extra nourishment, especially pretzels. I'm a dad who works part-time; in about an hour I'll pick up our daughter at her school, and we'll hang around the house for the rest of the day. It's raining today, so I'm writing this chapter instead of cutting the grass.

We have a lovely backyard, which I can see through the glass doors. Canada geese land in our yard and in the nearby pond. Behind our property lies a beautiful expanse of wild grass and flowers, which our daughter, Emily, identified as sweet goldenrod, elecampane, yellowwood sorrel, spotted touch-me-not, and others. Nearby stands a tall cottonwood tree that makes me sneeze in early summer and a very old willow. Once I saw a bald eagle in our trees! Whenever I do yard work, I try to learn from certain Catholic orders and use manual exercise as an opportunity for prayer and meditation.[1] Unfortunately I usually just grumble about my household chores. But I keep trying.

Family pictures decorate the living room bookshelves. Scattered around the house are keepsakes from places we've lived and souvenirs from places our family has visited. A number of antiques from my hometown also adorn our house. Everyone's favorite Vandalia antique is a coat hanger from an early 1900s merchant who sold "furniture, coffins, carpets, and window shades."

If writing ideas don't flow while I sit at the kitchen island, I move to the dining room or the front room. I love to work in the front room because my grandmother's old desk is there. For my morning spiritual reading, I sit in our brown chair and read from a prayer book and devotional periodicals. If the brown chair doesn't suffice for my reading, I move to another place. I'm rather like our two cats, both adopted from the humane society, who migrate around the house, resting in one room for a time then shifting to another place.

We don't know much about Jesus' earthly house. John 1:37-39 is a simple story about the place where Jesus stayed, but we get no details. Where did Jesus "crash," so to speak? Where did he keep his clothes (which, according to John 19:23-24, were nice)? Did he have his own place or did he lodge with others (for example, Mark 9:33)? Did he have "stuff"? One assumes not, or at least not very much. Did his neighbors complain about the crowds? Like Moses' grave, the place where Jesus stayed is probably best left unknown.

We know more about Jesus' land than his house. In his book *Landscapes of the Soul*, Robert M. Hamma writes how the commonplace images of everyday life abound in Jesus' teachings.

> It was of Galilee that he spoke in his parables: a place of rich harvests, of sheepfolds, and of vineyards . . . where sons went out, often reluctantly, to work in their father's

> fields, where a woman would sweep out her whole house in search of a lost coin, where people cared about that one sheep that had wandered off. It was a place where wolves ravaged flocks, where sheep and goats had to be separated, where brigands attacked lonely travelers. Lilies grew in its fields, flocks of birds filled its skies, fish abounded in its expansive lake.
>
> As he wove his parables of God's coming reign out of the seemingly insignificant details of the place where he grew up, the beauty of nature and the behavior of his countrymen spoke not only of their Creator, but of the saving action of God that was unfolding through his ministry.[2]

Think about home places that are special to you and how God touches your life in those places. It may be the home in which you live now, a home that was special to you at another time in your life, or an area or place that is special through memory or daily routine. How have special home places been important in your life? How does God speak to you in your home places? Can you weave "parables of God's coming reign out of the seemingly insignificant details," as Hamma puts it, from the place you live? How do you perceive God's grace in your life and the lives of people you know?

household sacred places

God speaks to us especially in our homes because they are extensions of our deepest selves. Here we feel protected and secure, but also vulnerable. Dick, a retired pastor who writes daily devotions at www.earlyword.info, notes, "Home is some kind of structure, be it a cardboard box or a two-hundred-room mansion. Home is also where our hearts find peace and rest. That is not dependent upon a physical structure. That is a relationship of trust with our Creator, Redeemer, and Sustainer." Diana R. Garland has written a book called *Sacred Stories of Ordinary Families* in which she discusses faith formation amid the crises, sorrows, and joys of family life.[3] In a chapter titled "Kitchen Linoleum as Holy Ground," Garland points out that God's presence breaks into our everyday challenges amid chores and household dilemmas. God meets us as we're cleaning house, supporting one another, and feeling at wit's end.[4]

A long, venerable tradition upholds home as a religiously sacred place. This is an area where many of us fall short; we are so busy, our families are pulled in so many directions, that we neglect to worship God in our own houses. In the Jewish tradition, Abraham E. Millgram writes, the home is regarded "as a shrine. This is not a poetic exaggeration, for the Jewish home was, in a sense, a little sanctuary. The family table was regarded as an altar, each meal was a holy ritual, and the parents were the officiating priests. Family worship accompanied many of the daily activities and transformed the biological and social relationships of the family into a spiritual kinship."[5]

Many of us do create specific sacred places within our homes: locations where we feel centered; God's love feels wide and close at hand. Tom H., a high school teacher, writes that his kitchen is such a place: "Here, I prepare meals for my family; thus it is here that I express my love for my family. It is also where I experience God's love and the wonders of the bounty God has provided for us." Author Frank McCourt writes of his grandmother's household shrine, a place in front of the fireplace where she prayed the Rosary.[6] My friend Cara, Grammy to eight girls, has a particular "wide place" at her house.

> The 1920s vintage rocking chair on my back porch, from my dear friend Lyda Ecke, is where I find joy and happiness. It is where I celebrate the wonders of my life and where I find solace. It is where I pray.
>
> I remember the day Lyda, then in her midnineties, called me to her house and insisted I take the rocking chair home. When I protested, she told me if I did not take it that day, she would give it to someone else! Having spent hundreds of hours in that chair rocking on her porch, I was not about to let it get away. Sitting in her

chair, I reminisce to myself about the good times we shared.

My heart overflowed with joy when, sitting in Lyda's chair, my son and his wife gave me the book *I'll Love You Forever* inscribed "To Grammy" to announce the coming of our first grandchild. The following year I was again in my chair when they told me a second baby was on the way. How blessed we were! Jon called barely a week later to tell us Lynn had miscarried. Fleeing to my chair, the memories and the agony of my own miscarriages came flooding back.

In the mornings I sit in my chair sipping coffee and watch the blue jays chase the songbirds from the feeder, and the squirrels chase each other in the trees, and I marvel at such beauty. I listen to the five wind chimes, in different keys, that tingle delightfully during gentle breezes and cause a cacophony during storms, and I think of the friends and family who gave them to me.

In the summer I love sitting in my chair after dark listening to the sounds of our nocturnal friends. Sometimes when sleep eludes me, I tiptoe to my chair and sit in the dark, solving the world's problems or just watching the world go by. As I sit in my friend's chair, I thank God for the wonderful life and blessings that have come . . . and I pray.

god in the rough times

Steve experienced a layoff at his job. A few years before, his oldest daughter had moved away, but Steve and his wife left her room the same, just in case she returned. He writes:

I walked around the house. My wife was busy at her work. Our only child still at home was at school. The phone was silent; nobody knows what to say to someone who was fired. Our dogs looked at me as though to say, "Aren't you supposed to be at work?"

I wandered around the big old house and opened the door to Patricia's room. I decided it was time to put her stuff in storage and take over her room so I could have a real office at home. For years I'd had a place in the basement with a desk, computer, and various other pieces of office stuff. However I'd never really liked to spend long hours in the basement. Patricia's room was huge, especially after I carried out all her unwanted stuff. I set up my work space just the way I wanted it.

Believe it or not, my home office is my spiritual place. I bought a set of classical music CDs and have the world's best music (at least that's what the label says) playing softly in the background at just the right volume with all the other knobs set just the way I like them. I set up my laptop computer with a new docking station and organized my computer files just the way I want them. Once the office was complete, I tore into finishing the book I'd been fiddling with for the past ten years but not really making much progress. It is now done and scheduled to be in bookstores within a few weeks. Two other books-in-progress and three manuscripts for future articles are now in just the right files within my computer, as is a ton of teaching materials.

Instead of spending eight to ten hours per day in the office [of my former job], I now spend as little or as much time as I want in my new "spiritual place." The completed book, written in partnership with a minister and an attorney, is all about making a difference in this world by connecting our work world with our spiritual world. I have worked through the various stages of dealing with such a career change to the point where I can now honestly say getting fired was the best thing that ever happened to me. It freed me to follow my calling in my spiritual place.

I've come to define a calling as a place where our talent, passion, and cause intersect. At times, when the words seem to flow, I look up from my computer in amazement to see the time is 3:00 AM and I've been

> writing for twelve to fifteen hours, unaware of the time going by. I now pity those who have to go to work and follow the drumbeat of others. I also now realize how ambition toward a career can be like a prison. Any of us can get so caught up in it we lose track of our true calling. Objecting to what someone further up the chain of command says is something we think twice or three times about, often deciding it is better for our career plans to keep silent. Eventually we are so invested in this career-path logic that we really don't see how we have sold our soul. My home office is my spiritual place where I rediscovered my calling and my soul.

God sustains us through rough family times, when our homes become, at least occasionally, difficult places. God continues to help us through the years. Sylvia, born in Hawaii, contrasts two homes—her childhood house and her college dorm.

> While I was young, my older brother, who suffered from schizophrenia, returned home from college on the mainland. During the Christmas season he underwent treatment for his condition. In the early '70s people didn't talk about mental illness. In an Asian family, mental illness was especially kept under wraps because it was viewed as a blemish rather than an illness. My brother resisted taking his medication and had attempted to commit suicide numerous times. One day around Christmas he had an episode where he became violent or tried to overdose (I'm not sure even what happened), and we had to call an ambulance to take him to the hospital. I remember sitting in the corner of our living room squeezed behind our Christmas tree. It seemed a safe place to hide to avoid all the confusion that seemed rampant in our household. The next year my brother was successful in a suicide attempt.
>
> God carefully orchestrated my spiritual growth! In my first year at college, I was challenged with the attempted suicide of a good friend. This was the year my past caught

> up with my present, and I was able to talk about my brother's suicide for the first time. God challenged me to make a choice: seek God or find comfort in earthly solutions. I associate my dorm with my spiritual growth. In my second year of college, I became a Christian, and I credit God with surrounding me with Christian friends in various walks of their spiritual lives and for giving me the curiosity to question what I saw and find answers to my burning questions on spirituality. Twenty-five years later I still have questions, but I'm so grateful for those years in the dorm as a new Christian.

god looks for us

At our home places God touches our lives in the most crucial ways—for here we most need help, guidance, reflection, rest, and restoration. Recall that parable about the woman who searched her home for a lost coin (Luke 15:8-10). The woman's place was simple and uncluttered compared to our own houses but imagine yourself digging between sofa cushions and looking under furniture for something valuable: a ring or an uncashed paycheck.

The image is perfectly understandable; who hasn't ransacked household clutter to find that essential, misplaced thing? We're like that essential item to God, says Jesus—something precious that calls for celebration when God finds us.

Amid your own cluttered house, how does God search diligently for you? What circumstances make you more "findable"?

God was even able to find my friend Martina under her bed!

> I grew up, the youngest of nine children, in a fairly small one-hundred-year-old farmhouse. You can imagine, it lacked many modern conveniences, most notably in the summer, air conditioning. The two upstairs bedrooms (one for the girls and one for the boys) were unbearably hot on summer afternoons and thus avoided until well after the

> sun went down. For this reason, when I was ten or twelve years old, I made the discovery that I could be entirely alone (rare in such a large family) if I stayed upstairs in the afternoons. The area under my bed was cooler than the open air of the room (shadier, I reasoned), and I would go there to read, play, and think. There I first felt the Lord drawing me to him. We were a churchgoing family but not open about spirituality. We had prayer books at home but no Bible. We allowed the church to tell us about our spiritual selves and didn't trust ourselves to know personal spiritual truths. But this particular summer, the Lord chose this time to reveal himself to me in a very sweet way. I felt God's kindness and love to me. I remember how the light was filtered through the pink chenille bedspread, and felt that same rosy glow within. I never told anyone why I went there, and when discovered one day, said I was just playing there because it was cooler. "You are so dumb!" was the appropriate-enough response! But I really believe God changed me that summer, making me more spiritually aware of myself and definitely more aware of his presence.

home countries

If I yellow-highlighted my typical weekly migrations on a local map, my comings and goings would cover a consistent area: our daughter's school this way, the grocery store that way, other favorite stores a different direction, my workplace another direction yet. My wife, Beth, and I both work, and our routes to work seldom vary. Our daughter has after-school activities that keep me driving to and from additional places.

Like my friend Tom D., whom I quoted in the previous chapter, I let the scenery speak to me. As I drive, I notice houses along my daily routes: small houses, pretty bungalows, newer styles. I wonder what is happening in the lives of people who live in the places I notice. I'll probably never set foot in these places; I'm only a passerby. Yet for other people these places are as crucial to personal identity as my own home is for me.

Author Wendell Berry reminds us that rather than merely working in a place, we should also strive to know that place and preserve it from thoughtless damage. Our home country becomes a loved, beloved place.[7] Around my community I see evidence of difficult economic times: the old rubber mills that once provided jobs and products, empty stores formerly occupied by major retail chains. I try to patronize businesses with local roots and support area ministries and arts organizations. I study the history of the community in order to appreciate its heritage.

I like my present location, not only because I'm comfortable here but because I'm happy and productive in my work and local service. I could live here a long time. A combination of circumstances, encounters, "the way things work out," and personal feelings make up a multifaceted, complicated response to places we live. In some locations, jobs plateau or don't work out; and the time becomes right for new adventures. A place may feel completely wrong: communities can disappoint; poor initial impressions linger; distressing circumstances arise that cannot be overcome. But a place can also linger in the heart as a wonderful home. I served only two years in my first parish, in Pope County, Illinois, before leaving to pursue doctoral work, but the location became precious to me because of the beautiful countryside and the wonderful people whom I was privileged to serve. Several of us still keep in touch.

The longer you live in a place, the deeper your sense of self is mapped out, so to speak, by that area. Malcolm, a retired construction worker and railroad enthusiast, writes about his community.

> I am grateful to God for having been born in Flagstaff, where I've lived for seventy-seven years. My wife was my childhood sweetheart and light of my life until her death in 2001. Our kids, a boy and a girl, were born, raised, and educated here, and every now and then I also thank

> God for the blessings God provided. From my home I can see the four seasons, each displayed on the San Francisco Peaks. My two kids help me "stay the course" through difficult times. My friends, although not large in number, are blind to my (many?) faults and steadfast in their loyalty. I am a fortunate man.

finding your center

People like me move according to available jobs, and others, like Malcolm, are rooted in a special place. (Malcolm is also a local leader in the historical society and has published many articles on railroading and northern Arizona.) My friend Karen, a writer and teacher in New England, has focused her priorities.

> Place has always been of immense importance to me. At an early age I knew I wanted to choose a place to live first, and then figure out how to make a living; the idea of having to follow a job to who-knew-where horrified me. That's not the usual career path these days, especially for someone with academic degrees, but somehow I managed. I live in a place I love, and I do what I love: write, play the piano, and make a home for my husband and daughter.
>
> My little corner of Indiana first found a place in my heart. My family lived in a small house on five acres. Those five acres included woodland, a swamp, a stream, a large garden, a horse paddock, several trees good for climbing or swings, and the foundation of an old barn, which yielded interesting artifacts to an aspiring archaeologist. Directly across the road lay a wider stretch of woodland belonging to neighbors. In every season except summer, when bugs and weeds discouraged me from playing there, those woods were my favorite place to be. During March and April the ground was covered with wildflowers. My great-aunt Mildred taught me their names: salt-and-pepper, bloodroot, lamb's tongue, crow's-foot, wake-robin, anemone, spring

beauty, Dutchman's-breeches, jack-in-the-pulpit, and mayapple. Purple violets grew thick along the road between my house and the Quaker meeting my family attended every Sunday. But once the mayapples bloomed, I knew that summer approached, and I waited until autumn frost killed the weeds before venturing into the woods again to swing on the grapevines, or just to explore, listening to the leaves crunch under my feet. In winter, a small pond in the woods froze over, and my brother and sister and I skated there. Snow collected in the vines that wound around the trees, making rooms and hallways for imaginary castles. Then when spring came again, I checked the woods daily, looking for the first flower to appear, the tiny salt-and-pepper.

Now that I live in Maine, about as close to nature as one can be and still have a house, I seek out new wildflowers: painted trillium, bird-on-the-wing, wild oats, goldthread, starflower, shinleaf, Canadian mayflower, rattlesnake plantain, trailing arbutus, pink lady's slipper. The land my husband's family owns, where all these wildflowers grow, has become as necessary to me as my Indiana woodlands were when I was a child. I barely survived two years in the urban East, out of easy reach of the woods. Moving to Maine was a relief and a homecoming. Here I can wander again, perhaps more at home in the woods than anywhere else, looking for wildflowers, listening to the wind and the birds and the leaves. Even the stone walls that climb the hills beside me seem to have grown from the earth, the shapes of the fields they once enclosed now hidden by trees. I feel centered, returned to myself, connected to all that is. Sometimes I repeat the words of Emily Brontë, who loved passionately her own corner of the earth:

> I'll walk where my own nature would be leading:
> It vexes me to choose another guide:
> Where the grey flocks in ferny glens are feeding;
> Where the wild wind blows on the mountain side.

What have those lonely mountains worth
revealing?
More glory and more grief than I can tell:
The earth that wakes one human heart to feeling
Can centre both the worlds of Heaven and Hell.[8]

The word *repentance* means "to turn around" or "to return." Repentance is a synonym for regret and restitution. But Karen's story, without using the word, points to a more positive meaning: of aligning one's priorities in order to remain true to one's values. Rabbi Bradley Shavit Artson writes that, "The beginning place, as with any return, is of having a place from which we start, a home base, a point of origin, a beginning." But Rabbi Artson also notes that turning/returning includes "finding our essence, . . . our core." He asks, "What is your core? What is your center? What is that part of yourself that you cannot abandon without walking away from who you truly are? Is your life balanced, centered? This kind of turning is not a turning to get back to some earlier time; it is a turning to remain true."[9]

childhood homes

For some of us, like my friend Martina, the spiritual journey began in childhood. Her journey has continued, though. For others of us, childhood was the time when we felt closest to God! We trusted God; our imagination was unfettered; we remained close to the natural world. (I'll say more about these themes in chapter 3.) In adulthood we began to question. The older religious answers no longer sufficed, but we couldn't immediately find a good substitute. Or we began our jobs and families and, without intending to, we drifted from God.

As you think about your own spiritual journey, perhaps you find insights by returning to the place you came from. That doesn't mean you have to readopt your childhood faith, which may or may not suffice for you now. But you can return to childhood landscapes—if only in your dreams, to paraphrase that old Christmas song—and understand afresh the important things that make up who you are, things that you cannot abandon if you're true to yourself and your spiritual search.

Anyone who knows me knows about Vandalia, the town where I was born and raised. My elderly mother still lives there, as do a host of friends and relatives. I've written two books about the town and still return frequently. It's the place I fairly automatically refer to as home, and then I have to explain that I don't live there. (No, it is not where they grow Vidalia onions, as people occasionally ask me.) Downtown Vandalia is quieter than the days of my childhood, though it's by no means dead. Vandalia's late-nineteenth- and early-twentieth-century commercial buildings remain, although the store signs have changed and a few downtown stores are gone. The old state capitol, constructed in 1836, remains Vandalia's symbol and pride. The excellent library, which I've patronized since I was three or four, operates next to city hall, and the familiar grain elevators still stand at Sixth and Gallatin beside the path of the old Illinois Central Railroad.

I gained a deep sense of history at Vandalia for several reasons. Simply going downtown provided me numerous historical sights: the dated cornices of the old commercial buildings, the historical plaques around town, and especially the old statehouse, where Lincoln served three sessions in the state legislature. History also had a personal aspect. Over thirty of my direct ancestors and many other relatives are buried in and around Vandalia; and when I was a little boy, I heard many stories about our family, especially when we made country drives on weekends. History, a sense of home, and rural vistas sentimentally mixed in my mind, so that eventually, history gave me a sense of joy similar to what C. S. Lewis describes as he recalls his reading of a favorite childhood story and poem.[10]

As I wrote earlier, the nooks and rooms of my childhood church also bequeathed me a deep sense of Vandalia. Church remained a huge part of my life—a changing, growing part—and strange as it may be, I love theological things because I loved local history first. If this life is so filled with old, dear things, what must eternity be like? What is older, more dear and close than God? Or, as Thoreau put it in another context, "Why has man rooted himself thus firmly in the earth, but that he may rise in the same proportion into the heavens above?"[11]

places of life's sacredness

Author Philip Sheldrake writes that home involves several things: a place where we pass through our stages of life, where we belong to a community, and where we have a relationship with nature and the seasons. He also notes that at our homes we experience the sacredness of life.[12] Paula, a pastor in Missouri, describes her favorite childhood place. I wonder if places like Paula's are closer to Sheldrake's thoughts than the homes we currently live in!

> Yes, my grandmother's house, the entire farm, was a wonderful place. Since I was a city kid, the farm was a place of adventure and fear. When we were little, we all had to go into the house if the bull got out, and my mom and grandmother had to get it back inside the fence. I was also not fond of some big white geese she had when I was small. I think that they were as big as I was. My grandmother had a huge garden, a pond, and lots of room to explore. When we were about eight and nine, my brother and I thought we found an old Indian trail. Turns out it was the cow path to the other field, but we thought it was cool. There were also cool things in the old granary. My favorite was a gizmo with a crank that you could put an ear of corn in and it would take the corn off the cob.
>
> My grandmother was a quilter and could make something out of nothing, so there were always old dresses or skirts of fabric trim around waiting to be turned into something else. Breakfast was always wonderful. She had homemade bread that was wonderful toasted and hand-churned butter from Blonde, her old cow, that we watched her milk, and homemade strawberry

> preserves. She let us sit at a tiny little table in her old kitchen and toast as much bread as we wanted for strawberry preserves and toast. My mother would come inside and tell her to stop it! She was spoiling us! And she was, but in the best way—she gave us herself.
>
> My grandmother's house was that wonderful combination of adventure, excitement, safety, and love. She lived in a house in a valley. And if we were coming to the farm at night she would have a really big yard light on for us to see. As we came to the top of the last hill on the old gravel road, it was always a contest as to who would be the first to see the light at Grandma's. It was the symbol of her always wanting us, always welcoming us. Her yard had a long rough lane to the house, and when we left she always waved good-bye to us until we were out of sight. Guess you can't tell how much she meant to me, can you?

Places like Paula's grandmother's become part of our history, our stories, our emotional and spiritual heritage. In a way, they remain secret places of refuge for us. Even our closest friends may not know about such places; when do hometowns and grandparents' farms ever come up in daily conversation, let alone in worship?

childhood places

Susan, a writer, historian, and editor, still has her childhood place, a house on Mill Creek Cove in Missouri. It continues to enrich and ground her adulthood.

> This place where I am holds tight to my heart, and has for as long as I can remember. A small stone house on the side of the Lake of the Ozarks, it was where we came to visit my grandparents for marvelous summer vacations when I was a child and teen. I remember swimming, waterskiing, fishing, learning to drive an outboard motorboat and then a speedboat, and having "lake friends" who we saw only

when they were also visiting their grandparents. Evenings were spent sitting on the porch in the dark listening to my grandparents and parents and their friends talk. Fond memories include walking up the gravel road to Joy's Dining Room, where twenty-five cents would buy a piece of pie and a chance to play the pinball game, or going to Joy's on Sunday noon or in the evening with adults for some of Faye Joy's wonderful fried chicken. The house was where we learned to play canasta with my grandmother, and launched into a lifetime of Scrabble games.

When I met my husband, I brought him to the lake for the first time on a gray, rainy, cold, October weekend. We didn't swim or boat or fish. I think we built a fire in the fireplace and read books and played Scrabble. Nine years ago, he and I purchased the house and began plans to add on so we could move permanently to the lake. About then, my godson decided to go to Washington University in St. Louis and then the University of Missouri Law School so he would be close to the lake.

Eight years ago my mother died suddenly. We were at the lake, en route to St. Louis for her seventy-fourth birthday, when my father called to say she'd had a fatal heart attack. Her spirit came back to the stone house. She is a comforting presence and has spoken to me at least once.

A year ago Daddy died in a nursing home in St. Louis. Through the time of caring for him—as my sister and I did—and taking over the business of his life, we found refuge at the lake, a place not only of peace and tranquility but also of a sense of safety that was the same as in our childhood.

I love watching for the heron fishing in the cove in the mornings, keeping the squirrels out of the bird feeders, and watching spring come to our little patch of woods. I lament all the changes that have come to my lake, from the million-dollar homes to the Wal-Mart Supercenter and Home Depot, but I guess it's okay. I carry my lake around with me, and it has as much to do

> with the summer I was eleven as it does with what I'm doing today.

Not all our childhood homes are houses. Jim, a retired public school teacher (and my own ninth-grade English teacher), remembers the seminary he attended:

> I was in the seminary for grades nine and ten, in Girard, Pennsylvania. The school was called the Divine Word Seminary, but it no longer exists, as it was torn down many years ago. It was (from the perspective of a young teen) a huge place: five stories tall with the dorms on the top floor, the classrooms on the second floor, and a gym and swimming pool in the basement.
>
> I have fond memories of that place. We went to church services twice a day. We were on the European model of schooling: we had Thursdays off, as it was workday, and went to school for half a day Saturday. On workday we were assigned various and sundry tasks. Once I had to mop five flights of stairs, and then got yelled at by the crew foreman, for I hadn't wrung out the mop properly. The tiny German nuns at Divine Word were tough as nails. It was not uncommon to see them fling two five-gallon milk cans over their shoulders and briskly take off toward the milk machines.
>
> One workday I saw my first farm animals up close and personal. The only exposure I'd had to pigs and cows was a little book I had as a young tyke, *The Color Kittens*. In it, pigs were cute and pink (piglets, actually) with little curly tails. And the cows were all calves. The first time I had farm duty, I was absolutely astounded, for the cows were bigger than I was and the hogs and swine were absolutely huge. And my first detail was to clean the pig poop out of the pigpen. Amen.
>
> Divine Word was a quiet tranquil spot, surrounded by an arbor of tall pines. We had a crazy biology professor who insisted we go bird-watching, an experience I deeply treasured later in life. That spring I saw some sixty-seven

different species of birds. Once I saw a hawk take a vividly red cardinal out of the top of a tall pine tree. (My love affair with chickadees also began at this time.)

I also vividly recall the night a fellow student went berserk: he thought he was a polar bear and went out in his pajamas to wallow in the snow! Next day he was nowhere to be found.

I was only there for two years. I dropped out when it came to my attention that there were women in the world as well as men. Academically, I thrived. Sophomore year I posted the highest average in the entire school (97 percent), although there were only ninety-eight students. I had an intense bout with homesickness while there but got past it. I had a wonderful time and received a fine education as well.

on the road again

My own most special childhood place—actually the most sacred place in my life—is one of family roots. Near Vandalia, Four Mile Prairie is a rural expanse of flat land—guess how many miles long—bordered by timber. My maternal ancestors settled this prairie during the 1820s, 1830s, and 1840s. Of course, I heard many stories of that area: the place where a great-great-great-uncle passed away in 1922, watching the world from his front porch; the place where a great-great-uncle lived his whole life in the same house and died in the same room in which he was born; the field where my great-great-grandfather was killed in an 1880 farm accident; places where our family's peach orchard stood before a 1920s winter killed it; the spot where six sweet apple trees stood beside a fencerow; the patch of ground where, in the 1910s, my uncle once found seventy-five mushrooms beneath a tree near "the old Frank Crawford place."

Driving Four Mile today, I take Route 185 and think about other places that are no longer there: a farmhouse where we visited relatives on holidays, a schoolhouse, and an antique shop that my parents loved. I also notice the country store where years ago I bought sodas in bottles and searched for bottle caps discarded in the gravel driveway, and I notice the small church that serves the area. I drive a little further and come to Brownstown Road, which forms a T intersection marked by a sturdy old tree. There the narrow highway curves and disappears into timber. Grandma Grace lived a short distance from Brownstown Road.

When I was thirteen, Grandma and I started a Crawford genealogy together. When she died, I continued the project and also copied all the inscriptions in the family cemetery. This was during my high school summers in the early 1970s, and so the joy of tracing my roots at Four Mile overlapped with my joy of being able to drive for the first time and having my first car (such as it was: a rusted, 1963 Chevrolet that had been my dad's stepfather's). I remember startling a visitor to the cemetery who hadn't expected to see a barefoot young man with nearly shoulder-length hair walking around the graveyard with a clipboard.

God never failed to lead me through varieties of experiences.

Nearly every time I visit Vandalia, I drive out to Four Mile. What do I gain from these drives? I feel nostalgia, certainly, and a sense of peace at the lovely setting with its rural ambiance; but also I renew a continuity with my past. And I feel a sense of gratitude to God for the experiences in which God has led me. If I were to encapsulate my own faith journey in a few words, I'd have to say that God never failed to lead me through varieties of experiences. God brought good from difficult or mediocre circumstances, sometimes veering me from paths I thought were best (and for which I'd sought the Lord's will) onto paths that were better for me. I've had no "earthquake" spiritual experiences at Four Mile, but when I visit that place, I'm grateful for the land and my journey.

Toward the end of the Torah, we find this passage:

> When the priest takes the basket from your hand and sets it down before the altar of the LORD your God, you shall make this response before the LORD your God: "A wandering Aramean was my ancestor; he went down into Egypt and lived there as an alien, few in number, and there he became a great nation, mighty and populous." (Deuteronomy 26:4-5)

The "wandering Aramean" was Jacob. Here Moses commands the worshiper to worship with a story about family and place!

The stories of the Israelite ancestors are unique, of course; we should never elevate ourselves to their stature in our own faith stories. However, Bible stories speak to us and teach us. We read them prayerfully and with humility and discover God's purposes in our own lives. If you came before the Lord God, how would you respond?

"A Midwestern farmwife was my grandmother, and she made churned butter from old Blonde's milk, and she made strawberry preserves, and she gave us herself. . . ."

"My family lived in a rural place, and I remember them as I drive along a state highway, and the road and the land remind me to live in gratitude to God. . . ."

the lord provides

My earliest memories are not of Vandalia but of the tiny community Bondville on Route 10 in Champaign County, Illinois. My family lived there when I was two years old (1959). In my first happy memory, I'm crossing the railroad tracks, calling to my mother, who's not far behind. We're walking to the post office on a pretty day. Unsure if I had genuine memories from so young an age, I returned to Bondville in the late 1980s and, sure enough, I recognized some of the places.

Mom once speculated what our lives would've been like if we'd stayed in Champaign County instead of moving back to Vandalia. It's an intriguing question, which many of us have asked ourselves: What if I had remained in X location rather than moving? What if I had made choice B rather than choice A that determined a big part of the direction of my life?

We sometimes use the word *providence* to describe God's care and direction. When the Bible was translated into Latin, the Hebrew words *YHWH Jireh* ("the Lord will provide," sometimes rendered *Jehovah Jireh*) were translated *Deus providebit*—and our English word *providence* comes from that Latin term.[13] When we think about providence, we affirm—or try to affirm—that God works in our lives for our good, moving ahead of us in order to create circumstances that help us. Even when we don't understand why something terrible has happened, God gives us strength in those times of deep need.

YHWH Jireh is actually the name of a place. In the story of Abraham and Isaac, Abraham "came to the place that God had shown him" and built an altar on which to sacrifice his son (Gen. 22:9). But after Abraham instead offered the ram that God did indeed provide, "Abraham called that place 'The LORD will provide'" (Gen. 22:14). The name of a particular location became a reminder to people that God helps and sustains.

YHWH Jireh was not a "home place." But home is where many people learn deeply that "the Lord will provide." God provides not only in blessings of food, shelter, and others but also by divine presence and help.

Thomas Merton concluded his autobiography, *The Seven Storey Mountain,* with a list of important places that preceded the monastery where he arrived at age twenty-six (and where he lived the remaining twenty-seven years of his life). If you read his life story, you see how each place became significant in his development and spirituality.[14] Reflect on your own life and consider how God brought you, metaphorically at least, from here to there to another home place to yet another, so that now, here, you are either far from God or very near. Consider how your early places are reflected in your current life. Who influenced you in those places? Look at the similarities and differences between your present home and your childhood home. Is your life, including your spiritual journey, true to your most basic values? How are you "centering" yourself at your home? Examine how God is helping, comforting, and challenging you at your present location. Can you affirm that God accompanied you from one place to another?

exercises

1. Draw a map of places you've lived or highlight them on a map. Use different colored highlighting pens to indicate whether a place was (1) wonderful, (2) just okay, or (3) terrible—couldn't wait to leave! In terms of your spiritual journey, would you evaluate those places in the same way?

   Then read Romans 8:28. How does that verse apply to the places you've lived? (It's okay if you don't think a certain place "worked for good" at all.)

2. In your notebook write at least two ways God has touched your life (and the lives of your family) in your home during the past year or two. Also list matters that you'd like God's help with.

3. Place a favorite household object in front of you—an heirloom, a book, or a picture. Write your thoughts and feelings as you look at the object. What does it represent to you about God, if anything? What does it represent about you and your "core self"?

4. Did you visit a special place during childhood? What was it? Write three or four paragraphs describing that place, similar to those quoted in this chapter. Or, if you prefer, draw a picture or write a poem or song about your childhood place.

5. Read John 14:2. The Greek word *monē* can be translated "mansions" (KJV), "rooms" (RSV), or "dwelling places" (NRSV). As a boy I thought of heaven in an amusingly small-town way, as a place with Victorian-era mansions up and down shady streets. How do you picture heaven? Don't worry if your images seem childish or outlandish; just see what images of an eternal home come to mind.

   Television shows about home design have been popular in recent years. Imagine yourself as a home designer for heaven!

3 abundant places

I've always loved Jesus' promise "I came that they may have life, and have it abundantly" (John 10:10). The Greek word *perisseia* means "abundance" and "overflow," and the similar word *perisseuma* means, basically, "leftovers"—extra food.

My dad was an excellent cook. He was a cook in the army in the Pacific theater during World War II. When I was little, he prepared huge meals—as if he still cooked for troops rather than the three of us: himself, Mom, and me. He'd say, "Why didn't you like it?" or "What was wrong with it?" if I could eat only one very large plateful. But if I truly did his cooking justice he proclaimed, "Paul ate six biscuits" with the same pride as he'd say, "Paul has a master's degree from Yale!" Cooking was his way of expressing and eliciting love.[1]

God expresses love for us through abundant life, but what is that exactly? The Hebrew scriptures describe longevity as a gift from God (Exod. 20:12; Ps. 21:4; Prov. 9:11), and yet even many years do not satisfy, for we're as transitory as any wildflower or creature on earth (Ps. 90:10; Eccles. 12:1-7; Isa. 40:6-8).

But Jesus offers abundant life, which is far more than just a positive attitude—forcing ourselves to feel happy and outgoing for Jesus when inside we're miserable and insecure. Abundant life is also different in the same way that a bland inner peace is different from "the peace of God, which surpasses [is more abundant than] all understanding" (Phil. 4:7). In the introduction we saw how God gives us abundant "roomy" grace, love, and safety instead of narrow places of distress (for example, Ps. 4:1). Imagine that you've entered a bright clearing or pasture after you've walked a treacherous path, or you enter a bright, expansive ballroom from a narrow hallway. Jesus gives you life—more life than you need, "extra" life, generous life that overflows, "wide" life. Such life includes the eternal life that overcomes the pain and sorrow of physical death. But Jesus' abundant life also precedes the grave: you have God's life right now, helping, guiding, instructing, convicting, and invigorating you, filling you with joy.

We've seen how home places ground us and root us. These same kinds of places can also provide parables of abundant life.

adventure places

Sometimes, when I'm back home visiting my mother, I daydream as I walk through the backyard of my childhood home. When we moved to the house in 1960, I was three, and our neighborhood was still fairly new. A neighbor's older house and barn had been the only places around, and so my backyard, while not a farm, still had a country feeling to it. The backyard is fairly long, with a spruce tree and two sheds my father built. I remember turning one of the sheds into a "no girls allowed" clubhouse, although my second cousin Jan, who lived next door, was exempted from that rule. The yard once had a sandbox and a swing set. Dad had a garden, much too large for him to manage well, considering his long hours as a trucker.

When I walk through the backyard now, I do not experience it the same way I did as a child. I've developed a sense of self that does not involve digging holes in the ground, battling dinosaurs (strangely prevalent in southern Illinois in the early 1960s), and slaying malefactors from outer space (ditto). Although I'm still a creative person, I no longer have the ability, expressed well in the comic strip "Calvin and Hobbes," to visualize an imaginative world as clearly as I perceive the actual world. For instance, I recall the terrifyingly high precipice that I scaled in order to save the town, far below the mountain, from a terrible avalanche. I also remember the same place as it actually was, a very small eroded spot on someone's yard across the street from my elementary school, which I, a bored patrol boy, mentally transformed into a marvelous place of adventure.

Four of Vandalia's several fine parks lie within close walking distance of our house. The closer park especially seemed a mere extension of our home, accessible by crossing only two neighbors' yards. Whenever a bunch of us kids got together, we played on the swing sets and slides, hid in the shelters, and dealt decisively with the aforementioned dinosaurs and space monsters. We also fished for crawdads in the gentle stream, using pieces of raw bacon safety-pinned to a line of string. Other times we played in the concrete pedestals of a long-ago water tower beside the Illinois Central tracks, loudly singing things like:

> Jingle bells,
> Batman smells,
> Robin laid an egg!

We howled at the sublimity of our wit.

One of the loveliest things that ever happened to me was the joy my daughter found in visiting those same landscapes. Many of Emily's childhood locations are sacred to me; and when she was younger, she loved playing in the Vandalia parks. We swung on the same swings, climbed on the same concrete pedestals, snuck into the adjoining park via the same gravel path beneath the trestle. One memorable afternoon—she was about seven and I was about forty—the two of us played in four different parks consecutively, as well as the playground of my elementary school! (I went to bed early that night.) She'll remember these places as "Grandma and Grandpa" places in a fascinating, faraway land, visited once or twice a year, rather than parks close at hand.

childhood places

The yard and parks were filled with all kinds of tantalizing mysteries, real and dreamed. How do the fireflies I catch in my hands on hot summer evenings make that light? How far away is the timber that lies beyond the cultivated field bordering our property? Where do the turtles come from before they stroll into the garden from somewhere, and do they ever leave their shells? What treasures might be buried beneath the spiky summer grass under my feet?

Recall places where your imagination soared like Superman—former schools, yards, or neighborhood streets. My friend Marianne, who works in education, writes:

> One of my sacred places is a wooded area of the farm where I grew up, in Robeson County, North Carolina. Some of my fondest memories are of those woods. In one area in particular there were four strange earth formations or mounds laid out like a square. The mounds were about seven feet tall. My dad, who grew up in the area, said they had been there when he was a boy, and everyone referred to them as "the Indian mounds."
>
> My dad and I would visit the mounds together and have incredible discussions, speculating who built the mounds and why: perhaps these mounds were made by aliens who had visited Earth! Sometimes I'd visit the mounds alone. I'd stand on top of one of them and look out into the great woods in all directions and yell out something I learned in Girl Scouts: "I-Zig-A-Zoom-Bo!" I

> was the queen of the universe, looking out on my loyal and adoring (if imaginary) subjects. Sometimes I'd stand below, in the center, with the mounds surrounding me on all sides, and I'd preach to the masses as if I were a young Billy Graham, or I'd deliver a Shakespearean soliloquy or sing a song or just sit there on the warm ground and listen to the rustling of the wind against the leaves, wondering what the future held for me while also clinging to the past, to this place of mystery. I felt connected to God in that place. I felt connected to the universe. I felt connections between the past, present, and future. It was always supposed to be my place eventually; that's what I was told as a child. But when I was a young adult, economic circumstances forced my parents to sell that land, which ended up in possession of one of my uncles and is now owned by one of my cousins. I know I will never see the mounds again, but somehow they will always be with me.

Brenda, a college teacher and freelance writer, remembers her elementary school.

> I grew up in the town of Jacksonville, Illinois, where I attended North Elementary from kindergarten through sixth grade. I spent more time in that one building than in any other school or college I have attended. It was and still is a special place for me. Some of my oldest and dearest friendships were made there. My first principal, named Joe Leiber, was blind. That was my first exposure to people with "disabilities." But even if I had been sent out into the hall in trouble, Mr. Leiber would walk down the hall and know it was me. When I answered him we would talk, and his disability would fade away.
>
> My fourth-grade teacher, Margaret Johnson, taught me that learning could be fun. She had a puppet made of foam that she called Cecil C. Serpent. She had made him at a teacher's workshop years before, but Cecil made learning come alive. He took part in our learning as he read stories, and we even gave him presents. I left that

year missing Margaret Johnson and Cecil. Even later, in junior high and high school, I revisited those friendships.

The playground at North Elementary also brings back fond memories. Much of the equipment is still there, and I can remember playing with certain friends. I remember the gym teacher had me and two other girls serve as "bird dogs." If we saw something going wrong on the playground, we reported it back to him, he checked it out, and we got candy and gum. So basically we were tattlers, but we sure felt important.

I go there now with my daughter and show her the old playground equipment and my old classrooms. I can tell her stories, but of course it's not the same as living the moment when life was simpler: when field trips to the local park or museum were big deals; when friendships would last forever; when teachers lived forever; when mortgages didn't have to be paid; when milk cost fifteen cents; when school meals were good; when you knew you would never forget this place and these special days. Those days were special. I have learned much from them. And I have learned much since. But I will never forget that special place.

faith like a child's

Childhood places are abundant places, places of imagination and vitality. I don't mean that childhood has no problems and responsibilities; childhood is filled with many difficulties and pressures. If I pause to remember, I can still feel the hopelessness and anxiety that certain tough kids elicited in me, even though, if I saw those people today, we'd be cordial and I'd certainly not fear them. The beloved comic strip "Peanuts" was, in part, based on recognizable facts: children's cruelty to one another and the heavy despair of rejection and failure that visits us when we're old or very young.

But in childhood we're under someone's care—hopefully someone who is good and loving and responsible. (Of course, this may not necessarily be so.) As children, we have time—time to play and dream, time to waste. No one judges us on our skills and productivity. In adulthood we shoulder our own yokes and burdens, even get used to them. Our religious faith may become hardheaded and self-reliant—in other words, different from what faith could be: spontaneous, trusting, generous, and expansive.

We have only one story of Jesus' childhood, the well-known story of Jesus in the Temple (Luke 2:41-52). In several passages the New Testament depicts harshly the Jewish teachers of Jesus' time. But in this story they clearly care about Jesus! Since he lingered in the Temple for three days, the leaders must have fed him and tucked him in at night. They enjoyed his company! Little-kid-Jesus sounds impatient with his parents, using the same exasperated tone that children use when grown-ups seem so foolish! "Did you not know that I must be in my Father's house?" he asks Mary and Joseph, who spent three hellish days searching for him (Luke 2:49).

Children receive the kingdom with eagerness and enthusiasm.

But—I'm admittedly speculating here—perhaps Jesus had that experience in mind when he said, "Let the little children come to me; do not stop them; for it is to such as these that the kingdom of God belongs" (Mark 10:14). The Jewish leaders had not hindered little-kid-Jesus, even though his parents didn't understand. He too wanted to take time for children.

Furthermore, Jesus notes, "Truly I tell you, whoever does not receive the kingdom of God as a little child will never enter it" (Mark 10:15). How does a child receive the kingdom? With trust, you might say, with dependency, with openness. Children receive the kingdom with eagerness and enthusiasm, the joy of discovery, an unabashed sense of mystery. Children would experience Jesus' love without second-guessing his sincerity. In Marianne's words, Jesus would become the place where they connect with God and the world.

In certain ways, we should not remain as children! Growing emotionally and in experience is essential to maturity; no one enjoys adults who demand—like a toddler or adolescent—that the world instantly address their needs. Too, children have short attention spans. They can focus intensely yet "move on" quickly. When she was very young, my daughter had great friendships that lasted a little while—for a summer perhaps—and then she made other friends, scarcely missing her former playmates. As a little boy I was the same way. Adults who flit from friend to friend or from one cause to another, don't seem to have a strong center.

Paul warned, "When I was a child, I spoke like a child, I thought like a child, I reasoned like a child; when I became an adult, I put an end to childish ways" (1 Cor. 13:11). The key word is *childish*, which differs from *childlike*. Paul himself had childlike qualities: he was affectionate and genuine rather than calculating (1 Cor. 2:3-5; 2 Cor. 2:4; 1 Thess. 2:5-8); he was sensitive and solicitous (1 Thess. 3:4-5); yet he didn't demand that people focus on his needs first (2 Cor. 1:3-6; 11:9; Gal. 4:12-14). He trusted God and wasn't ashamed of that trust (Rom. 1:16). He focused intensely upon his task (2 Cor. 4:16-18; Phil. 3:12-14). He even wore his heart on his sleeve (2 Cor. 2:4; 6:12); he expressed sadness when he was misunderstood or lonely (2 Cor. 2:3-4; 2 Tim. 4:9-11). Certainly he depended upon God first and foremost, and not, as do most of us adults, upon his successes, resumé, belongings, or self-sufficiency. Reading his letters, I doubt that Paul was an easy person to deal with! But neither are little children.

Paul also had *joy*—a word he often repeated in his letters. Dr. Donald Demaray of Asbury Theological Seminary writes that laughter and joy have a strong role in a healthy religious faith as well as in personal health. Demaray notes that children begin to laugh at a very early stage. If a child's parents display a good sense of humor and a positive perspective, children will likely continue to have good humor and joy as they grow into adulthood.[2] As for us adults, says Demaray, we lose our childhood joy thanks to many reasons: a false sense of dignity, a sad outlook gained from stress, even a feeling that joy and humor are somehow unreligious. But laughter, he writes, is a highly appropriate response to our salvation. To recognize God's great love for us, in spite of our failures and good intentions, makes us smile and experience childlike joy.[3]

barefoot days

If you're like me, memories of certain places in your life make your feet feel good. I think of the hot concrete outside the Vandalia Dairy Queen; the cool kitchen linoleum of a friend's house; the grass of the park; the sticky softness of tar-patched streets in summertime; the blessedly cool aisles of the grocery store; the gritty texture of the beach at vacation spots and the shock of the waves when I first waded in. Sometimes as a teenager I offered to run errands for my parents, partly to be helpful but partly to be out and about with nothing on my feet. The sidewalk in front of the library and city hall felt warm, like a concrete patio.

We adults usually don't set forth from our homes barefooted with the goal of a fun-filled day. But I still like to go barefoot when I feel a little silly and also when I'm feeling sad or bored or need to change my perspective. In one place where we lived, I pushed Emily in her stroller to the neighborhood market, both of us barefooted and hungry for M&Ms. It's been said: "If I had my life to live over, I would start barefoot earlier in the spring and stay that way later in the fall. I would go to more dances. I would ride more merry-go-rounds. I would pick more daisies."[4] When I'm older, I know I won't regret the silly, spur-of-the-moment joys that bring a kind of healing.

Sometimes I'll still see people driven barefoot by summer's latitude. One time I noticed a shoeless dad herding three or four sandaled kids through our local Kmart. Another little family, obviously big team fans, arrived at a baseball park for an evening game and stood in the concession line. The dad and kids wore shorts and sneakers, but the blue-jeaned, ball-capped mom had bare feet. Do such parents cry and whine to go barefoot while the kids retort, "No, you'll catch cold and then you'll have to miss work"?

Places where we pull off our shoes may not be holy ground, but they shine in our memories. Just the simple act of discarding shoes after a big work day is enough to fill the heart with peace. I've a friend who keeps warm at home in wintertime with sweaters and sweatshirts but definitely not shoes and socks: "I can't relax unless my feet are comfortable!"

A number of years ago, Maxie Dunnam wrote a book called *Barefoot Days of the Soul*, in which he compares the joy and peace of God's grace to the first days of spring when children finally can go barefoot outdoors after the long confinement of winter.[5] That's a nearly perfect image for the joy of God's grace! (If you don't like going barefoot, substitute the image of a pair of comfortable house slippers.) Often, if not most of the time, we take God's grace for granted. God loves us, has forgiven us, and is taking us to heaven when we die. We know these things by faith and carry on, just as we know the sun will rise. At key times, however, the enormity of God's love "hits" us. We really don't have to earn God's love. Nothing separates us from God's love. We have absolutely nothing to fear from death. We truly are deeply loved by God. What an overwhelming relief!

Do you think of God's grace as something that frees you from your sadness, your feeling of being "stuck" and confined? Does God's grace free you from your self-importance and from the burdens life has handed you (or you've handed yourself)? Do you feel relief, deep in your heart, by God's grace?

childlike joy

Continuing the general lines of these thoughts, think about the activities you love to do outdoors. Maybe you like going barefoot outside. Or maybe you like to take hikes or play with your kids or grandkids. Perhaps you love to play a sport: you're crazy for softball; you have a permanent volleyball net in your backyard; or you can't wait to toss around that football each fall. I know golfers who, if it was their last day on earth, would play a round. Maybe you like to sit outdoors and paint or draw or write, or you like to go boating. Maybe you go outdoors by yourself and sing at the top of your lungs. Think about how happy that makes you feel—then ask yourself if your faith gives you anywhere near the comparable joy.

Emily and I go sledding on our hill in wintertime. Sometimes we speed all the way down; sometimes we get bogged down in heavy, wet snow and tumble over. When life gives you bad snow for sledding, make snow angels. I'm well into middle age; I look silly on a sled, but I don't care. We have fun! We have memories—memories of sledding in winter, making leaf piles in autumn, and enjoying the warm weather of spring and summer. Such times and places as these live in the heart for many years—more than meetings and chores and have-to tasks.

While a student at Yale Divinity School, I usually left my dorm room door open except at night. I liked to have people to drop by. My room was next to the first-floor entry. One evening, a friend stood at the entry watching a substantial, late-autumn snowfall. Such a snow wasn't uncommon in Connecticut; but my friend, who grew up in Florida, had rarely seen snow. We chatted for a few minutes, and then I returned to my reading. I felt tired and overwhelmed with studying—a typical feeling when you're in school.

Lost in thought, I was startled to feel a snowball hit me in the head as I sat at my desk. Barely throwing on a coat, I chased my friend outside, and we fought with snowballs for several minutes in the darkness.

Returning to my room, cold but sweaty, I realized my feelings of sadness and tiredness had completely disappeared! A short time outdoors did the trick.

The Bible abounds with images of newness and renewal: "He put a new song in my mouth, a song of praise to our God" (Ps. 40:3); "Every day I will bless you, and praise your name forever and ever" (Ps. 145:2); "Those who wait for the LORD shall renew their strength, they shall mount up with wings like eagles, they shall run and not be weary, they shall walk and not faint" (Isa. 40:31). Many people find God's renewal best when they're outside. Robert M. Hamma's book *Earth's Echo: Sacred Encounters with Nature* is one that assists people in attuning to God's presence outdoors.[6]

"how great thou art" places

Many kinds of places make us feel close to God. My friend Michael, a university professor, writes:

> I always feel the spirit and presence of God outdoors. My wife, Deborah, and I are part of a hiking club at our church, and the organizer also feels God outside. He tends to select hikes along water of some kind. Being in the wild with the sound of water is very relaxing to me at the inner, "primal" level. However, it makes me energetic at the same time. My best prayers/answers seem to come to me when taking the time to "be still, and know that I am God!" (Ps. 46:10).

Michael adds that, because God is light, he feels God in the natural light outside. His story reminds me of the hymn "O Worship the King," which contains the lines:

> O tell of God's might, O sing of God's grace,
> whose robe is the light, whose canopy space
> . . . .
> Thy bountiful care, what tongue can recite?

> It breathes in the air, it shines in the light;
> it streams from the hills, it descends to the plain,
> and sweetly distills in the dew and the rain.

KB, a retired executive, is a Midwesterner by birth. He and his wife moved to the South. He describes connecting with God in this new location:

> A favorite place? Rocky Face Mountain in northwest Georgia! Having been raised in the plains of rural Illinois, I find that God is revealed in inspiring ways in these mountains. Our home where we now live is uniquely positioned looking down across a valley and up at Rocky Face Mountain. Each morning time, I have coffee with God in our sunroom, watching the mountain's silhouette slowly reveal its majesty more distinctly with each second of the sunrise, just as God's majesty becomes clearer as we focus on the Spirit, Jesus, and Jesus rising from the dead.
>
> My time with God's mountain inspires my faith by divine grand design, from the magnificence of the view as well as through the complex community of living things, all intertwined purposefully with a rhythm and harmony.
>
> Sometimes low cloud formations interfere with the view of the mountain, just as the world around us can interfere with our relationship with God. I am reminded that God is always there, always unwavering, and always loving.
>
> Sometimes as the sun burns off the fog that hinders our view of the mountain, I am reminded that Jesus can burn off the fog that hinders our relationship with God and others.
>
> Sometimes the mountain's majesty is revealed by bright sunlight, just as Jesus brightly reveals God's love for us. And each time, as I have coffee with God, I am reminded that like the complex purposes of the mountain community, I have a purpose in loving God and in making a difference each day, as God again opens a divine world

> of opportunities and responsibilities to me. I am reminded that, like Rocky Face Mountain, God is always with me.

Kym, a university administrative assistant, writes about the sea:

> When I was younger, my family owned a home in Miami Beach, and we vacationed there several times a year. One year, when I was about seven years old, my parents took my siblings and me to the beach early one morning. The sun was just rising and the ocean was calm and beautiful against a cloudless blue sky. After standing there admiring our glorious view for a few minutes, my mother, who is a devout Catholic, knelt down, pulling us all close to her, and whispered, "God is here." I can remember initially I was afraid, thinking God was here to take my family to heaven, but after a few moments, I felt very calm and at peace, and I actually felt God there with us.
>
> I am an adult now and still vacation at the same beach every year with my children, where I have told them the same thing my mother told me when I was a child.
>
> No matter where I am in my life, as soon as I stand there and look out into the sea, I find God and feel the calm as God lets me know that all is right in the world.

My hometown friend Tammy, a banker, has a wonderful memory of a time she felt close to God outside:

> Back in the late '60s and early '70s, First Baptist Church of Vandalia had an "awesome" youth group. We called ourselves YPC (Young People for Christ). Our leaders opened up their house and their lives to more than fifty young kids, year after year.
>
> The closest I felt to God was during one of those Sunday night events. That particular evening, we were hosted by a couple out on Route 40. At that time their place had a small pond and waterfall. We all sat outside on the hillside and gave our testimonies. The summer night sky was filled with stars. We sang the song "He's Everything to Me."

> Looking at the sky with all its stars was one of the most peaceful, fulfilling, safe, and faith-filled experiences I have ever had. For me God was sitting right there with us that night. We all felt close to one another and to God in that outdoor setting, with good food and stars in the sky.

Regions and areas speak to people differently. In chapter 1, I quoted my Ohio friend Stacey, who connects in spiritual ways to the Rocky Mountains. I've a friend from the Carolinas. She worked most of her career in Arizona and then retired to Colorado. When she visits the Carolinas, the region no longer speaks to her as strongly; she's now accustomed to the trees and terrain of the West.

being outdoors

Other kinds of outdoor places draw our attention. Byron Crawford (no relation to me) is a columnist for the Louisville, Kentucky, *Courier-Journal.* He writes movingly of Kentucky people and locations. In one column he writes about his "secret pond," a place that he found near Stanford, Kentucky, when he was a boy. "There was a peaceful, soothing atmosphere about the spot, enhanced by its obscurity and by my memories of that enchanted first visit in the snow." He carried in his mind the image of that pond for nearly thirty years. Eventually he decided to see if it was still there. He wasn't sure he could find it—or if he did, perhaps it had changed. But he found the pond, and it looked the same!

> I stood for a moment just looking at it, and liking it, feeling the restfulness that always descended on me here.
>
> Had twenty-seven years really passed since I last stood here, wearing my four-buckle overshoes and with snowflakes in my eyelashes, reveling in the sight of a glorified mud hole? . . . I wondered if I was crazy, coming here on New Year's Eve in weather like this to visit a pond.

> No, I was all right, I decided; it's just that I don't turn loose of yesterdays very easily.[7]

Perhaps, like Byron, you're drawn to waters. My friend Bev, who works for the state of Indiana, recently took a trip to Florida. "I visited a friend who lives on a lake. He just let me relax and piddle around. I sat on the dock and crocheted most of the afternoon away while watching nature: God's playground. No schedule to be at a certain place; it brought peace to my soul and helped clear my head so I could make certain life-changing decisions."

Perhaps you've a tree that is sacred to you, whether as a personally special place or as a place where God touched your life in some way. The poem "Rowan Tree" by Lady Carolina Nairne (which I discovered on Hollie Smith's CD *Light from a Distant Shore*) speaks of "hallowed thoughts" that attend one's memories of favorite trees.[8] My friend Sylvia remembers her childhood home in Hawaii.

> My peaceful place was a little corner of our lot where a stone wall met a fence my dad and I had built together. Here there grew a tree that provided shelter for a number of birds. From this spot I could look across the valley to the mountain on the other side but also got the cooling trade winds from the north. At dusk a bird or two would visit this small tree, and I would hear the songs of the shama thrush or an occasional cardinal or mynah bird. At sunset the spot would get the last orange rays. Every now and then the breeze would carry the aroma of my dad's little orange blossom tree or the ginger flowers in our backyard.

My mother loved a pawpaw tree that grew on land between her childhood home and the one-room school she attended. One time she and Grandma and I walked to that property—it seemed to me we walked for miles. Mourning doves gave their haunting call. Finally Mom found a gnarled root she believed was part of the long-ago pawpaw tree. I'm sorry that I probably couldn't find the place again.

Yet it remains a sacred location in a personal sense; I often return to that tree in a memory of the happiness of the woods on a pretty childhood afternoon.

A tree figures in one of my favorite movies, *The Shawshank Redemption.* Inmate Andy Dufresne, serving two life terms for murder, remembers an old tree in a hay field where he had proposed to his wife. He never calls it a sacred place, but he tells his friend Red that if Red ever gets out of prison, he should look for something Andy buried beneath that tree. Years later, Red keeps his promise to Andy. In despair, unable to adjust to freedom after forty years in prison, Red visits the tree. What Red finds there, in the shade of the tree among sounds of birds and insects (and Thomas Newman's gorgeous score), occasions his redemption.

Outdoor places can bring us wonderful renewal, redemption, and happiness, in more ways than one could describe, in many meanings of the word *sacred.* I'm leaving out a whole range of religiously sacred locations in the world's religious traditions: places of water like the Ganges River and the Jordan River, as well as sacred trees and outdoor shrines where religious pilgrims gather. Native American spirituality certainly honors the earth and the earth's creatures. In Latin American countries many religious festivals involve an outdoor procession with lots of flowers and music.

I had a friend who much preferred walking in the woods to going to church. I understood his feeling; churches can be uninvolving and predictable, but nature provides tremendous variety, beauty, and possibilities for discovery. My advice to my friend was to, if possible, find a church he liked, because God's Word, the sacraments, and congregational fellowship are essential for a "whole" spiritual journey. A risk of prayer, whether solitary or congregational, is that you might be talking only to yourself! But you also shouldn't abandon meditative, prayerful times of solitude and contemplation. Those are the times when we think creatively, our emotions become peaceful, and we are freed from the trivial distractions that blind and upset us. Thus the promptings and leadership of God's Spirit can become clearer to us. Although Jesus used an indoor image when he discussed solitary prayer (Matt. 6:6), he often prayed outdoors (see Luke 6:12), alone with God.

places of daily routine

Unlike these outdoor sacred places, other kinds of places fill our time but do not necessarily engage our identities and relationships in a significant way. Such places include airports, hotels, highways, supermarkets, our sitting spots in front of the TV, and so on. These places are part of our routine but not our stories.[9]

Recently Beth and I were stuck for eight hours at the Dallas-Fort Worth airport; you'd be amazed at the pleasant conversations you can make with total strangers when you're all in the same predicament. Normally, though, most of us isolate and insulate ourselves while attending to our business in public places. We become harried and selfish. That slow driver? That elderly lady who holds up the express lane of the grocery? They're just trying to aggravate me! So is the traffic light that turned red when I was in a hurry: it saw me coming! I'm being humorous, but you know what I mean. When I'm out in public, sometimes I fall into an "it's-all-about-me" attitude.

In chapter 2 I discussed places that make up everyday comings-and-goings: the roads I take to work, the locations where I shop, my favorite stores for errand running, and so on. I try not to allow my daily chores and deadlines to define me; I don't want to look back on my life and see only to-do lists and deadlines. The contemporary poet Stephen Dobyns wrote a haunting poem called "Short Rides," in which a man, who has to keep several important appointments, accepts rides from the devil, who (driving a great car) never brings the narrator to his intended place on time. The poem ends, "life slips by in a succession of short rides."[10]

I've a friend who, like me, enjoys shopping. When I was new to northeast Ohio, she and I e-mailed about good places to shop. Unlike many men, I feel content—almost spiritual—when browsing among stores. Admittedly I do shop "like a man," purposeful and a little rushed, but shopping does make me feel happy and peaceful. But is this actually a spiritual feeling? Not really! I feel happy, even grateful to God, when I am in places of no particular spiritual import. Yet my feelings of contentment might be blinding me to actual spiritual promptings.

Because of busyness or thoughtlessness, we let these kinds of places blind us to a proper order of our lives. For instance, James writes, "Come now, you who say, 'Today or tomorrow we will go to such and such a town and spend a year there, doing business and making money.' Yet you do not even know what tomorrow will bring. . . . Instead you ought to say, 'If the Lord wishes, we will live and do this or that.' As it is, you boast in your arrogance; all such boasting is evil" (4:13-16). The prophet Amos similarly cautions against the false security of abundance (6:4-7). Although work, money, and home maintenance are important, we need a growing, faithful relationship with God to bring our joys and tasks into perspective. We need God, who can help us when the rest of our lives are falling apart.

god in the routine

Because God takes the initiative in our spiritual journeys, we should add that any routine place can become a place of spiritual import too. To say otherwise would be to deny the promptings of God's Spirit to empower us as they will.

> God breaks into our everyday chores and errands in many ways.

God breaks into our everyday chores and errands in many often quiet ways. When I was about nine years old, Dad and I went together into G. C. Murphy's, where Mom worked prior to my birth. Murphy's was a wonderful, all-purpose store, that sold all kinds of toys, games, cloth, candy, and household products. Dad suddenly declared, "Paul, it's time you had your own Bible!" I was startled, for at that time in our lives, Dad seldom went to church. I suppose he wanted to have some role in my religious training, which in our family was wholly Mom's faithful initiative. The store also sold Bibles, and Dad and I picked one out, which I still have, an undated King James Version published by Word Publishing House of Cleveland, Ohio, with its pliable leather cover and two-columned text, each verse separate. I might have picked out a red-letter edition if I'd known of such a thing, for my favorite color is red. I considered reading that Bible cover to cover, but I didn't get very far. Those "begats" have scared away many a well-intentioned Bible reader! Although I didn't begin reading the Bible seriously for many years, that little event was a genuine starting point in my spiritual life.

Another personal story: I once had an experience of sudden comfort, joy, and clarity in a parking lot as I walked from my car to Kroger, the grocery chain I frequented at that time. I had a potentially serious problem about which I was obsessing. Outwardly I was fine, but inwardly I could not calm myself of worry and "what if" thinking. As I walked, something clicked in my mind and heart. Suddenly I felt at peace. I'd sought that peace desperately, and because I sought it, it came. But I could not will it into being, and it didn't come on demand. It was an "aha!" moment when everything fell mentally and emotionally into place.

Many people would leave it at that, a moment of quiet intuition. But I believe the Holy Spirit helped me clarify my thinking and put away my anxiety at that point. My distress returned off and on, but never as strongly, until the problem was resolved about a year later; and I never lost that initial sense of peace and trust.

Should I have built an altar to God at that spot like Jacob at Bethel? No (and it surely would've gone against Kroger's rules). But the parking lot became a place of God's help.

A lovely story comes from Victor, a university administrator:

One would never think that a simple sidewalk could be a place of significance, but the sidewalk outside of Lipscomb Hall at the University of Georgia is very significant to me. I went to school there for all of my degrees, but while there as an undergraduate, I was like most students and learned more about myself than imaginable. I went to UGA as one who had attended church all of my life. Every Sunday. Without fail. Rarely missing. To be honest, I enjoyed church and the faith I thought I had at the time.

One simple evening just as any other, I was leaving Lipscomb Hall after dinner to go study at the library. As I got to the sidewalk heading to North Campus, I saw a fellow student coming toward me that I had seen from time to time. We never talked to each other but always shared the cursory nod and "Hey." But this day was different. He stopped me and simply stated, "I see you all the time here on the sidewalk and you seem to be such a happy person." He went on to say, "But I have always wanted to ask you a question. Have you ever accepted Christ in your heart—fully and unconditionally?"

Of course, I was totally caught off guard with not only his question but his boldness for Christ. Something in me wanted to tell him that I was a church-going person from day one and that he need not waste his time on me. Yet something even stronger told me I could not answer his question with a resounding and unqualified "Yes!" So, I looked at him and almost with shame said, "I really do not know." We prayed together, and at that moment on that very spot on that very sidewalk, for the first time in my life, I felt I (not my parents for me) accepted Christ in my life—fully and unconditionally.

Even after I moved off campus from Lipscomb, I often times revisited that spot—for my own personal reasons. While later working at UGA, for all the years I was there, it was not strange on a really tough day or during some rough times to find me there just to be there. That one concrete space still, to this very day, empowers me in

> ways it is hard for me to explain. More than anything, it reveals the simplicity of Christ and how Jesus can come in and totally change our lives.

Even though our lives become filled with everyday kinds of places, we can remain open to God's possibilities and cultivate a sense of God's providence as we go about our daily business. We can give God the "elbow room" to work in surprising ways. (God always has "elbow room," but we don't always perceive it.)

abraham and job

The Bible provides examples of "faith in everyday places." One is Abraham. In Genesis 21 Abraham and the ruler Abimelech discuss a well seized by the king's servants. The text does not elaborate on what exactly happened, but Abraham gives the king sheep and oxen to prove that he, Abraham, had actually dug the well. That place became known as Beer-sheba, which means "well of oath" (or possibly "well of seven," referring to the seven ewes of vv. 28-30). Abraham also planted a tamarisk tree and invoked God's name there. In this brief story, we gain some meaningful lessons. For one thing, Abraham worshiped God in connection to a business contract. He did not separate God from his everyday dealings and problems.[11] Second, Abraham's transaction showed respect for the place itself. Why did he plant a tamarisk tree? Those trees made good windbreaks for orchards, so the tree had practical as well as symbolic use. Abraham did not disregard the place where he conducted business; he improved it.[12]

Another example for our faith is Job, though in a way unrelated to his sufferings. In chapter 29, Job laments:

> When I went out to the gate of the city,
> when I took my seat in the square,
> the young men saw me and withdrew,
> and the aged rose up and stood;

the nobles refrained from talking,
    and laid their hands on their mouths;
the voices of princes were hushed,
    and their tongues stuck to the roof of their mouths.
When the ear heard, it commended me,
    and when the eye saw, it approved;
because I delivered the poor who cried,
    and the orphan who had no helper.
The blessing of the wretched came upon me,
    and I caused the widow's heart to sing for joy.
I put on righteousness, and it clothed me;
    my justice was like a robe and a turban.
I was eyes to the blind,
    and feet to the lame.
I was a father to the needy,
    and I championed the cause of the
stranger. (Job 29:7-16)

The city gate is a venerable, often overlooked "place image" in the Bible. Look up *gate* in a good Bible dictionary, and you will find a lot about these places. In ancient times, the city gate was the place where all matters of significance took place. People conducted legal transactions there, got the local news, and shopped. Markets were located there, as well as judges hearing cases. Officials issued important announcements at the city gate. To say they "push aside the needy in the gate" (Amos 5:12) means that the poor were abused and not given justice. The expression "the gates" refers to the city itself (Ps. 87:2; 122:2), a synonym also applied to hell in Matthew 16:18.[13]

In this passage from Job (as well as the remainder of chapter 29), Job recalls the prestige that, amid his calamities and illness, he has lost. He does not brag about his "popularity." He regrets the losts of his community standing!

My father stressed the importance of having a "good name." In a small community where everyone knows everyone else, being a trustworthy, responsible person who keeps promises is very important. People today worry about their credit rating: do those computer records, stored somewhere by people who don't know me, reflect well on my character? Having a good name means having character and integrity. If I say I'm going to do something, you know I'll do it; and if for some reason I can't, you know I'll try to make it up to you.

Job is proud of his character. Both the upper and lower classes honor his name. And yet his speech moves beyond "character" in the sense of virtuous. His community standing is not limited to his reliability, economic status, or his conventional religious practices. He serves others in need. The basis of his character and community standing is Job's service to others.

Job's speech deepens our sense of what place means. For Job, the place of the city gate stood metaphorically for a whole, righteous way of life: People honored him because he worshiped God, but he worshiped God by serving the sick and intervening for the despised and neglected. We speak of giving certain people "space": people who are strange and different to us, people who are poor and unfortunate. How would you react if a homeless or intoxicated person came into your church during the Eucharist? Job included all people in his space, because that was also God's space. Job's presence in public places reminded people of God, who also is concerned for the poor and misfortunate.

How can we judge the spiritual worth of our favorite places according to Job's standard?

abundant life

Earlier I wrote about my father's big meals. My family had several good cooks, including Grandma Crawford. When the family got together—we three, Grandma, and Mom's brother and his family, plus great-aunts and great-uncles and their families—everyone brought food, and Grandma and the women cooked some more. I made mashed-potato-and-gravy lakes on my plate and with an evil crash of my spoon sent the gravy flowing, wiping out the green beans. Everyone in the family barely saved room for dessert, as if the earlier words "Bless this food" would gain us God's overflowing favor. Some of the family lingered in the kitchen and cleaned up. Others went outside and discussed world events, while still others collapsed in front of the televised football game.

Jesus poignantly notes, "Your ancestors ate the manna in the wilderness, and they died" (John 6:49). Grandma's farm reminds me of Jesus' saying; only my mother and several cousins and I remain of those large family get-togethers. Food nourishes the body and the soul, but someday we'll die no matter how much food we eat. So my childhood place reminds me of the many blessings God provides for us.

In John 6:1-15 we read John's version of the "feeding of the five thousand." Jesus provided an enormous meal for an enormous crowd. There were leftovers, twelve baskets of bread, although apparently everyone gobbled up the fish. Naturally the crowd sought more. But instead of more food, Jesus offered them the bread of life—in other words, himself. In giving bread, Jesus offers everything we need for life, if we define "life" more broadly than just our physical stamina. He provides God's grace and help. He provides access to God for our prayers. He provides guidance and assistance. He helps resolve some of our problems and adverse situations; others he does not, but he remains fully present for us as we bring our needs to God. He provides us life forever with God.

God has become known to us in the person of Jesus. God approves us before we realize, gently drawing us to Christ and teaching us. God has taken the initiative to provide sustenance sufficient for this life and the next. To each of us God gives special places that remind us of God's wonderful, abundant life.[14]

exercises

1. Write a story or poem or song about your favorite childhood place. What adventures did you enjoy there?
2. Write a description of your favorite outdoor place, similar to the stories in this chapter. Include any experiences of God, no matter how subtle (or even corny), you may have had at that location.
3. Planting a tree or special plant provides a sense of continuity. When we recently moved, we brought along a cutting from a favorite mint plant. A tree can memorialize a loved one, a lost pregnancy, or a significant milestone. Plant a tree or bush or flower to commemorate an important event in your life, including a spiritual breakthrough or an answered prayer.
4. After you read Job 29:7-16, take an honest inventory of your social "righteousness." Are you perceived as one who cares actively about others, as one with character?
5. Do something silly or out of the ordinary today. Put on your pajamas before supper or do jumping jacks in the middle of the living room or lie in the grass or go outside and talk to a squirrel or dog or whatever! Think about how Christ sets you free to rejoice in life (Phil. 4:4-9).

4 sorrow and solace

During my childhood, my parents and I regularly shopped in St. Louis, about seventy miles away. Those were the days when downtown department stores still prospered. Urban St. Louis was overwhelming to a little kid from a small town: the smells of fish, fruit, and bus exhaust at Union Market; the shouts of street venders; the sounds of inner-city traffic and '60s rock and roll. The Gateway Arch, which at the time consisted of two unfinished legs of metal, seemed a grotesque entry into the city. I could not imagine being abandoned there. But one time, in the toy section of Kresge's, I momentarily became separated from Dad. I panicked, for I needed him but had lost sight of him. A weight of despair settled on me for a second or two; what would I do without my parents' help and protection?

Recall Psalms 42 and 43 again. When the poet asks, "Where is your God?" he does not ask a theoretical question about God's being. Nor does he raise a point of scriptural interpretation. The psalmist knows God exists and that God can be counted on. Honest in his distress, the psalmist *wants* God. But for the time being, God seems missing. The psalmist feels a double despair because of his situation and because of God's seeming unavailability. The latter is worse.

Trouble finds us; we feel struck down and confused by circumstances. If God helped me with such-and-such problem, why doesn't he help me with this other, more serious issue? Why does this trouble that I have (illness, family conflict, a job loss, or whatever) seem more powerful than God's grace? Where is God when I need God? Why doesn't God answer my prayers? Certain places speak to us of trouble rather than peace and safety.

grandma's farm

Grandma Grace was sixty-seven when I was born. I knew her as a tiny little woman who kept her white hair under a hairnet night and day, as if she hoped to save it, as she would the good china, for a special occasion; and if none came, nothing had been wasted. My memories of her are a litany. She was very loving and also opinionated and "set." But she was devout in a way I liked. She wasn't "showy" about her faith. She didn't parade her biblical knowledge or argue points of doctrine to make herself appear right but took seriously the Lord's admonition to do good in secret and to trust God's unfailing love. She always drove, always had a car; this woman who never had indoor toilets or a washing machine sped down the road in her light green '49 Ford. Widowed in 1954 after forty-six years of marriage, she stayed with us in town quite often but preferred her own home.

She died in her sleep in a late-night house fire that destroyed her home when I was fifteen (in 1972). If things had turned out differently, I could have kept her farm, described earlier as a place of roots, childhood wonder, and abundance. Her farm still holds those kinds of memories for me. I loved to roam the place: the two old barns that stood near her house, the hills and dales of her property, the trail that led to her small pond where I shot at enemy airplanes with the loaded end of a fishing pole. Even the car door of a 1937 Chevrolet, which had been unaccountably used to patch a hole in a wire fence, became transported in imagination as a gateway into magical places. I also explored inside Grandma's home: the cluttered kitchen with its tall, battered cabinets; the pump that brought the only water into the house; the old calendars that hung behind Grandma's aprons and rags within her sunny, dusty pantry. I liked Grandma's rough-textured, burgundy sofa; her father's well-worn rocking chair; a table in the corner piled with local papers, her purse, and pocket items; the front bedroom, with its four-poster bed and lumpy mattress; the tall, walnut wardrobe filled with linens; and the corner bedroom, where figurines stood, dusty, upon a small vanity. Most of all I enjoyed the sunny corner family room. While the grown-ups talked, I sat alone in that room and read and thought. I read the Pilcher family history, which Grandma's cousin Blanche had compiled in the 1930s, and the theological books written by C. C. Crawford, a distant cousin. I liked the possibility of becoming someone who writes theological books. Grandma bought me a pictorial Bible dictionary I still use, including doing the research for this book.

Memory exacerbates grief and, in the case of a house fire, memory of beloved objects reminds you, painfully and arbitrarily, of what happened. What became of Mom's old guitar? Oh . . . it was in Grandma's attic. Wouldn't it be nice to have my great-grandfather Pilcher's chair? Yes, but it sat in Grandma's living room . . . Remember those pretty figurines? . . .

I thought I'd handled Grandma's death well, except for a strange reticence to speak of it and a pessimism, a heavy perplexity that emerged at odd moments. Adolescents are long on self-consciousness and short on productive introspection, and I went about my schooling and my career. But fourteen years later, nearly to the day, the space shuttle *Challenger* exploded. I could scarcely contain my rage—rage at God, rage at circumstances. I lived in Virginia at the time. Foolishly

I got in my car and drove. A certain hilly vista along I-64 near Ivy, Virginia, always gave me peace. I traced my feelings back to an earlier, more personal rage and finally faced what had happened in 1972.

The delay was not difficult to understand. I saw my grandmother alive one Sunday afternoon, and then I never saw her again, alive or dead. The following Thursday night she literally disappeared from the earth. Like the prophet Elijah, she was taken up into heaven. Without the dreadful tasks of an open-casket visitation, then dividing goods and discarding clothing—all to make the loss seem hard and real—Grandma's death never seemed believable.

I never saw Grandma again, but I saw her house "die." And although my grief at Grandma's death was delayed, I have always, in a real way, mourned the house and felt cast down by its violent end. Sporadically over the years, I returned to the farm, hoping to enjoy walking the land again. But although I walked the property several times, I couldn't overcome my sadness and allow the farm to become part of my adult affections. Finally we sold the land.

As I mentioned, I love to drive Route 185 across Four Mile and think about Grandma and my subsequent journey. At the risk of sounding facile, I can tell you that Grandma's death taught me never to take life for granted! Over the years I've asked myself, *What legacy would I leave if I died today? How would people remember me? Should I be kind or harsh in X situation?* I've striven for a balanced personal and professional life focused on serving others as well as spending excellent family time. I also make time for friendships. Tragedies can awaken us to proper priorities, and in my case my priorities were set fairly early.

Psalm 73 assures us of God's continuing presence to those of us struggling with difficult questions. The psalmist has nearly lost all confidence and faith, and yet God is near: "Nevertheless I am continually with you; you hold my right hand. You guide me with your counsel, and afterward you will receive me with honor" (73:23-24). It was a humbling experience when I realized how many blessings I'd received from God during those years when I resented God bitterly, although unconsciously, for allowing my grandmother to die as she did.

difficult places

Many places in our lives are demanding; they're places we avoid. They're not wide but narrow, distressing. If we can't avoid these places, we feel uneasy, upset, filled with unpleasant memories.

As I began this project, I e-mailed several friends to see what kinds of locations of personal importance came to their minds. Most recalled comparatively happy places, as I would have. Why should I ruminate, after all, on a place for which I've bad memories? The junior high hallway where I was punched by a bully as a crowd looked on? The intersection where I hit a van that had run a red light? A motel room near Pittsburgh where my wife and I waited two days, delayed from urgent business, because our car had broken down over the weekend and no garages were open? A place where a job didn't work out in spite of my best efforts?

These places are minor compared to the difficult places of some people. Some people have miserable childhood homes, horrible family situations, nightmarish places. My father told me stories of the battles of Leyte and Okinawa during the Second World War: stories of combat, gruesome deaths, days when, in his words, "You didn't care if you lived or died; you just wanted it over." Several years ago I taught a world religions class at a Kentucky prison. About twelve of us met in a smoky classroom in the educational building; the men took classes for their college degrees; it was a good class. During break, one tall student spoke about his interest in the class and his own explorations of faith and theology. Towering over me, he suddenly asked, "Have you ever been incarcerated?" I said that I hadn't. He just shook his head, looking bleak.

Think of difficult places: a crime scene, a place where you were robbed or raped, a place where you were abused, a place of terrible squalor, or a place where you felt trapped and abandoned. Clearly these kinds of places linger in our hearts too.

A certain place in Vandalia brought sadness to my father's voice. Dad and his father, Andy Stroble, were together downtown when Andy collapsed in front of a now-long-ago barbershop on South Fifth Street. That was 1935, when Dad was twenty-two and Andy, dead of a stroke, was fifty-two. Dad lived until 1999 and always recalled that place where his father collapsed. Reading his tone, I believe my grandfather's death was harder on my father than his World War II experiences. He'd survived combat with a certain pride, a grim amazement at what he'd seen and overcome. But his father's death seemed a sadder memory.

So it is with many of us as we recall certain places and events. *Closure* is a popular term these days. Is there really such a thing? We may come to a sense of acceptance about a person's death, but we never "close" that person off in our hearts. Sometimes we speak of closure when we mean, "I'm uncomfortable with your pain; I don't want to take time to understand your feelings; and I'd feel better if you 'moved on.' " Fortunately we needn't worry about God becoming impatient if our feelings are slow to heal—indeed, if they never fully heal.

wilderness places

The word *wilderness* has both positive and negative connotations. In the Bible, *wilderness* refers to grassy areas (see Ps. 65:12), dry places (Isa. 43:19, 20), desert regions (Ps. 107:40; Deut. 32:10; Job 38:26), or specifically the inhospitable area of the Dead Sea (2 Sam. 1 2:29).[1] In our ecologically aware age, we think of wilderness as places that ought to be preserved (and perhaps already are). Even in the positive sense this word *wilderness* holds urgency: human beings should not develop and use every natural place they find.

Wilderness rings authentically as a spiritual metaphor. Looking back on my own life, I think of situations where I was confused, discouraged, and under pressure. I wasn't happy and didn't see what the future held. I felt tested; I wasn't sure how best to deal with a situation and couldn't quite perceive God's presence. In other cases the test required strength and perseverance. I associate certain locations of my life with those times of stress and testing.

Some of my wilderness situations involved waiting: for medical tests results, for news about school or job applications. The most painful places of our lives can be, temporarily at least, the mailbox (postal or e-mail) or the telephone. When life is unhappy in an nonspecific way, we can distract ourselves with other activities. But anxiety, "what if" thinking, and distress plague us when we wait.

Yet waiting on God is a positive thing—according to the scriptures. "Those who wait for the LORD shall renew their strength, they shall mount up with wings like eagles" (Isa. 40:31). Some of us, when we wait for the Lord, are not mighty eagles but rather squawking blue jays or fussy killdeer! "Lead me in your truth, and teach me," prays the psalmist, "for you are the God of my salvation; for you I wait all day long" (Ps. 25:5). "Our soul waits for the LORD; he is our help and shield. Our heart is glad in him, because we trust in his holy name" (Ps. 33:20-21).

The Israelites' first experience with wilderness did not go well. In fact, the wilderness experience was a shock to Israel. (The Torah from Exodus 15:22 to the end of Deuteronomy concerns the Israelites' forty years of wandering, but for now, read Exod. 15:22–17:7). Following the Exodus, Moses led the people from the Red Sea to the wilderness of Shur (Exod. 15:22). Unfortunately the people went for three days before finding water at Marah—but the water was bitter and undrinkable. At that point the people complained against Moses. The NIV translates that verb as "grumbled" and the RSV as "murmured." After all, three days is a pretty long time to go without water! I would've murmured vigorously.

As important as water is, the greater issue was the trustworthiness of God. The Israelites were saved from the Egyptians, but for what? Wilderness is not cultivatable; no one can make a living there.[2] It was as if God had promised the people something fine and wonderful but, in the meantime, gave them a poor substitute, just to tease them. Moses shortly "cried out" to the Lord, who in turn showed Moses a piece of wood that sweetened the water. But the Lord took the opportunity to warn the people (Exod. 15:26); God would provide for their needs—and indeed, water is an immediate, crucial need—but God also requires their faith and obedience.

The people encamped at Elim, with palm trees and twelve springs of water (15:27). There is no record of the people's conversations at this point; Elim is a good place. But when they moved into the wilderness between Elim and Sinai, the complaining started again, and worse. Not only were the people hungry, but they wished they had died in Egypt! Better to have died in Egypt than to get so far only to perish from hunger. God again showed completely trustworthiness, yet the people disobeyed (16:20, 27). Trusting God in a crisis situation isn't easy.

Trusting God in a crisis situation isn't easy.

The people moved farther along, to Rephidim, perhaps in a southeasterly direction from the Red Sea crossing. At Rephidim the group made camp—but there is no water at Rephidim. Once again the people complained to Moses, and interestingly Moses did not cry to the Lord for help, as in 15:25, but responded angrily to the people. When Moses did beseech the Lord, it was for protection rather than for the people's need for water.

The Lord provided Moses a solution: take the staff with which he struck the Nile, and as the Lord stands before him at the rock at Horeb, Moses must strike the rock, which will provide water. Moses did as instructed. But the text goes on to discuss Moses' new name for the place: Massah and Meribah, or "test" and "quarrel" (17:7).

The people had asked, "Is the Lord among us or not?" and their impatient questioning is memorialized.

The faithlessness of Israel is a repetitive theme in the Torah, but we should not be appalled at how the Hebrews responded. Instead we should "learn from history" and ask how we also stumble and return, grumble and repent, many times in our own lives. My own Massahs and Meribahs dot the map; many times I've struggled with anxiety and questions. Most of us grumble about things far less important than actual hunger and real thirst; we grumble when our feelings are hurt or when our work goes poorly or when other people fail our expectations. We also grumble when serious crises emerge; like the Israelites, our faith becomes sorely tested.

God is trustworthy, but we habitually grow fearful when our prayers seem unanswered, when God's promises seem delayed or withheld, and when circumstances go badly and we don't know why. If we're honest, we memorialize those places where we lost confidence in God.

places of burial

One of the sad stories of Genesis is in chapter 23; Sarah lived to be 127 and died at Hebron (Kiriath-arba) in Canaan. Abraham mourned her, but none of us can mourn a family member without immediately shouldering responsibilities. Weak and brokenhearted, we must think clearly, move forward, and make the arrangements to honor our loved one who has died.

In Abraham's case he had to negotiate with the Hittites for a burial place. He and Sarah were not natives to the land but sojourners. Filled with grief, Abraham dickered for a tomb. According to the customs of the time, negotiation was standard. The Hittites treated Abraham with respect and offered a sepulcher as a gift. But Abraham wanted clear title to the land. Finally Ephron the Hittite sold Abraham the cave at Machpelah for four hundred shekels, and

Abraham buried Sarah. The sojourner in Canaan owned a sad piece of property. Eventually he, Leah, Rebekah, Isaac, and Jacob were buried there too (see Gen. 49:31). The site is still a holy place; a Muslim mosque now stands at the site, for Islam also honors the Hebrew forebearer.[3]

I remember the slightly morbid process—humorous in a way—of selecting my parents' burial place with them. The issue was not the price of plots but the scenery. My mother liked the view from a certain place in the cemetery where she could see from that high point the Vandalia statehouse (the old state capitol), the steeple of the United Methodist Church, and other buildings such as Allen's Furniture and the Liberty Theater. In autumn the view is especially beautiful as the trees appear in full color. That spot was Mom's "sacred place"; she liked to drive there and look at downtown Vandalia. Mom is elderly and cannot write any longer, but if she could, she'd tell you about this pretty vista and the perspective she gained there as she faced various challenges.

"I don't know if I can see the statehouse from here," Mom said as we strolled that day among available plots on the hill.

"Yes, you can," I responded.

"I think I could see it better here," she said, ruefully noting that her preferred spot was "taken."

"But this plot is just as good," I assured her. "The view of the statehouse is excellent."

"I suppose so," she responded.

"You won't see anything when you're buried here!" scolded Dad, impatient to finish.

As we considered plots, a woman approached us with the surprising offer of selling us her plot and tombstone! Apparently she'd preplanned her funeral and then changed her mind. The location, though, didn't have a good view of the statehouse, so we declined.

We settled on a good spot in the cemetery with a lovely view of downtown. An unpleasant chore was accomplished. About a year later, as I drove through that cemetery, I noticed the tombstone of the lady who'd offered us her plot. She'd passed away! Her original plans had sufficed.

I've always loved cemeteries. "Paul likes to visit graveyards, even when he doesn't know anyone there!" declared Dad, sounding as if I crashed strangers' parties. My mother's family cemetery is located in a peaceful, wooded place near Four Mile. Ancestors back to great-great-great-great-grandparents are buried there. When I was a little boy, we decorated graves on Memorial Day. I would trot back to the oldest section that dated from the 1830s. My favorite tombstone read, "Moses Cluxton, Sen. Died March 13, 1855. Aged 56 yrs 10 ms & 4 d." His name was carved much smaller than the date of death; I thought that was cool. Another surprisingly clear stone read, "SACRED to the Memory of Comfort Williams, Who Died March 30, 1847, Aged 54 Years." Eventually I discovered that she is my ancestor.

My mother is still alive, but I visit my dad's grave regularly, at the place we selected with a view of the statehouse. That cemetery, a beautiful, hilly place in Vandalia, is one of the highest points in that part of Illinois. But visiting his grave is difficult, unlike my visits to the graveyard near Four Mile. While I honor the memories of my ancestors, I miss my father. I remember both the good and the strained elements in our relationship. I wish certain things had been different, but I'm also glad we grew closer during my adult years, for some people do not have even that.

My friend Victor experiences strong feelings when he visits his own father's resting place:

> Riverside Cemetery in Albany, Georgia is a unique place for me. Many of my family members are buried in Riverside. We can all share the many feelings that a graveyard can produce: fear, a sense of history, peace, and so on. But, Riverside provides a different perspective for me. You see, Riverside Cemetery is divided into two parts separated by what used to be a road. Both sections are

> fenced on all sides to appear as different cemeteries. What is unique about the other section of Riverside is that is was for whites only. Although I went there often to bury family members while growing up, I often found that my grief was mixed with my desire to know why we could never bury "my people" in the other section.
>
> After so many generations of my family finding final rest there, when my father died in 1999, we were able to bury him in the other section of Riverside—the side for whites only. It was such a healing process for me because of my strong disgust for racism. I was happy more so because it seemed so stupid to me that we as human beings could not even die and be buried without separating ourselves from each other. My father's death was a healing process for me in many ways, but I left Albany a few days later knowing that the greatest last tribute my dad could have had was to have done what he did, maybe not in life but in death. That cemetery has significance in my life not just because it represents the sins of our past but also the hope that we can find, if we wait long enough, in the future.

For Victor, his cemetery is a place of hope that God can heal even absurd and sinful things like racism. But God needs time—and like Moses or Victor's dad, we may see only glimpses of the promise.

places never to forget

My mind recoils at statistically small tragedies from the evening news—three people killed in an accident, eight people killed in a house fire, a young child raped and killed. Because I teach history, I routinely read about terrible places and events that I cannot comprehend: approximately 24,000 fell in a single day at Antietam in 1862; 57,000 British troops fell (a third were killed) in a single morning at the Somme in 1916; 20 to 30 million or more Africans perished in the course of trans-Atlantic slave trade; 27 million people in the Soviet

Union perished in World War II; and on and on. When we read about the Holocaust, places like Auschwitz, Belzek, Sobibor, Treblinka, and others serve as eternal reminders and memorials to what happened.

Similarly, I can name other places that evoke sadness, horror, regret, reverence, and other strong emotions. Places like Wounded Knee, Vietnam, Columbine, the World Trade Center. Battlefields like Verdun, Passchendaele, Okinawa, Iwo Jima, Chancellorsville, Gettysburg, Vicksburg, and many others. I think of people who have experienced massacres and genocide—Armenians, Cambodians, the Kurds, and others—as well as epidemics, such as the plague of the fourteenth century, influenza in the early twentieth century, AIDS in our own time. Leafing through a history book evokes tragedies that make any sensitive person astounded and confused at the world in which we live.

Even statistically smaller tragedies force us to ask, Where was God when this happened? Or we may say: Why did God not prevent this terrible thing from happening, assuming that God exists?

Certain places raise hard questions about God's power and human suffering. The Bible itself does not avoid them. Why did God take so long to remember his covenant with Abraham, Isaac, and Jacob as the Israelites suffered in slavery (Exod. 2:23-25)? Why did God harden Pharaoh's heart until the death toll in Egypt mounted (Exod. 5-14)? Why did the birth of Jesus result in the killing of babies, making holy Bethlehem a crime scene (Matt. 2:16-18)? Read the book of Job in detail; Job himself gives us ample permission to ask tough questions. The Psalms do too; some are quite frank in asking God, "Why?"

> "Has his steadfast love ceased forever?
> Are his promises at an end for all time?
> Has God forgotten to be gracious?
> Has he in anger shut up his compassion?"
> And I say, "It is my grief
> that the right hand of the Most High has changed.
> (Psalm 77:8-10)

Since we're human and finite, we don't understand why terrible things happen. We cannot conceive of any possible reason for certain tragedies. We know God is always present to people. He always hears prayers. He always offers us grace, guidance, and hope. But . . .

After long bouts of questioning God, Job finds himself in an uncomfortable position: God turns the questions back to Job. God may do the same for us. As I write these words, I know I'm a decent person. I say to myself: *I would have saved Jews; I would have protested the slave trade; I would have stood up for injustice. . . .* But would I, if push came to shove? I hope so, but would I take a stand against evil if it cost me my predictable routine, my home, my family, or my life? Am I really different from the people who let African slavery or the Holocaust happen? Terrible places not only numb us with their horror but distance us from what happen. "They" did that awful thing to "them."

The problem is not that you and I are personally culpable for events like the Holocaust or African slavery, but we're part of a world in which great suffering is possible. We are heirs of staggering examples of evil—and we're capable of condoning great evil. John Donne's statement "No man is an island" has become such a common saying that we've lost the power of its truth: we are all diminished by one another's sufferings. We let suffering happen because of our lifestyles, our indifference, our busyness, and our goals. We absolve ourselves of any necessity to help. We thereby take steps away from God.

The Bible also teaches that God can be known within terrible events: the massacre of Hebrew babies (Exod. 1:15-22); the horrors of exile (Isa. 40:1-2); the loneliness of a childless, elderly couple far from home (Gen. 15:1-6). For Christians, God is known in the sufferings of Jesus: look at the crucified Jesus and you know something about who God is in the world. But this is a mystery we take easily for granted. God may be hidden and unrecognizable, but God is there, in spite of everything, present with us, still worthy of our worship.

the god who sees

In terrible times and places, we ask God for help. We trust in God. The Israelites asked, "Is the Lord among us or not?" because they already believed!

Read Genesis 15–17 and 21. Ten years after Abram and Sarai settled in Canaan, they still had no child, in spite of God's promise (Gen. 15:4; 16:3). But Sarai had an idea: "You see that the LORD has prevented me from bearing children," she said to her husband, "go in to my slave-girl; it may be that I shall obtain children by her" (Gen. 16:2).

Many times we struggle to know and to do God's will during times when not all the facts are in. Sometimes we must act and ask God to lead us. In the thinking of ancient times, childlessness was divinely ordained. Therefore, letting Abram bear Sarai a child through a "surrogate" made sense. On the other hand—if an argument from silence is valid—the couple did not specifically seek God's direction in this. Sarai made up her mind that this was the solution. Abram "listened to the voice of Sarai" and Hagar conceived.

Verse 3 indicates that Hagar became Abram's *ishah*, which can mean either concubine or wife. As such, she could not be sold; nonetheless, she was still Sarai's servant and not a household equal.[4] In this situation, household relationships became tense. Sarai changed her mind; she perceived Hagar felt contempt for her, which was perhaps Sarai's way of coping with her own unhappy feelings. She told Abram, "May the wrong done to me be on you!" or as *The Torah: A Modern Commentary* translates, "The wrong done me is your fault!"[5]

Seemingly passive in this situation, Abram did not protest or take a stand. He simply gave Sarai her household prerogative. How else to get rid of Hagar but to mistreat her so she will leave on her own? Hagar too believed that removing herself from that situation was the best option, and so she fled into the wilderness. But at a spring, the angel of the Lord appeared to her and sent her back. The angel reassured her, "I will so greatly multiply your offspring that they cannot be counted for the multitude" (Gen. 16:10). Hagar's child's name was to be Ishmael, or "God hears," for the Lord heard her distress and responded (v. 11).

Not merely a victim in a domestic soap opera, Hagar was an important character. Following Eve, she was the first biblical woman to whom the Lord appeared. Furthermore, she was the first person in Scripture to name God "El-roi" (v. 13). The original meaning is obscure, but the phrase seems to mean "God of seeing." The following phrase is also obscure but may mean, "Have I really seen God and remained alive after seeing him?" The place where the Lord appeared to Hagar became known as Beer-lahai-roi, or "the Well of the Living One who sees me" (v. 14).

That is not the end of the story. Hagar returned, but the enmity between her and Sarah continued. (By now, both Abram and Sarai had received name changes from the Lord: Gen. 17:5, 15). Years later, Sarah disliked Ishmael playing together with Isaac (Gen. 21:9-10). There must have been several years' age difference between the two boys, but they were half-brothers, after all. Sarah's unhappiness boiled over and she ordered Abraham to "cast out this slave woman with her son." Verse 11 understates, "The matter was very distressing to Abraham on account of his son."

God, however, instructed Abraham to do as Sarah wished, essentially because both sons were children of God's promises for great nations. Hagar must have wondered why she was sent back to the household only to have matters come to this? Think of analogies in our own time. Why does a person work hard on a marriage, only to have the spouse leave? Why does a person put in long years at a difficult job, only to be laid off? Why does a person build a strong business, only to have unforeseen circumstances (economic downturns, road construction, a corporate competitor) ruin dreams? Hope is difficult to find in such situations.

After Abraham bid Hagar and Ishmael good-bye, they wandered in the wilderness for an unknown time—until their water ran out. Hagar despaired of her child surviving and placed him a distance away. If he died, she couldn't bear to hear his cries.

But true to the child's name, God heard. A Jewish midrash puts it this way, "God hears Ishmael's cry 'where he is.' God always hears and judges man on his present circumstances, not for where he was or will be."[6] God called to the stricken mother and reiterated his promise to her. "What troubles you, Hagar? Do not be afraid; for God has heard the voice of the boy where he is. Come, lift up the boy and hold him fast with your hand, for I will make a great nation of him" (vv. 17-18). In chapter 3 I discussed the relief we feel when God touches us at key moments. Hagar discovered, again, that God is faithful.

Interestingly, she was all the while near water, even though she hadn't noticed before (v. 19). Surely there is a great lesson in that verse; when our situation seems most desperate, God may show us a temporary or permanent solution. The text does not elaborate much more, except that Hagar and her son settled in Paran, the wilderness area south of Beer-sheba in the east-central Sinai region. According to the text, she "got a wife for him" from her homeland, Egypt. (The Koran accounts of Abraham's family are slightly different, with more material concerning Ishmael, but Muslims honor both sons of Abraham as persons of faith.)

> When our situation seems most desperate, God may show us a solution.

What places function for you as a Beer-lahai-roi? What situations did you bring on yourself? Which ones brought you intolerable pain? When were you victim of someone else's hostility? Where were you when God saw or heard your despair? How did God give you perspective? How did God assure you that there was a larger context to your problem than you could perceive?

places of hopelessness and hope

Amid the difficulties and sorrows of life God touches our lives with places of hope. Some places bring healing in more ways than memory; they become mental and spiritual places that facilitate health. My hometown friend Linda writes:

> I was there again today, that place I go when I'm looking for serenity and peace.
>
> This special place dwells in my imagination and yet it is real. East of my home, the land rises gently from a small unnamed creek to Hickory Hill, where shagbark hickory trees dot a hilltop sprinkled with pines and multiflora rosebushes. It is here I found my special place.
>
> In February 1999 I was recovering from the first intravenous chemotherapy treatment for breast cancer. Several weeks earlier my friend Chance had given me a couple cassette tapes to listen to while I rested.
>
> I had them for several weeks when one day I slipped a tape into my player and listened as the voice told me to imagine a place of peace where sunshine could reach the ground unobstructed. My mind immediately envisioned the gentle rise between Hickory Hill and the creek. This became a spiritual place for me.
>
> Once I realized that alternative treatment for cancer was something I wanted to pursue, I was led—that's the only way to describe it—to a holistic doctor. In one of our first sessions, the doctor told me to close my eyes and imagine a special place. Then imagine God—however I understood and named God—standing in front of me, smiling. Since I'd already visited my "special place," in the blink of an eye I was there, bathed in God's love.

> I have visited my "place" over and over again while the cancer returned, twice. I was there again today and as always, came away recharged.
>
> You too can go there. Close your eyes, and imagine . . .

Other places remind us of God's specific blessings. My friend Bill, a World War II veteran, remembers a time from his own youth when quick thinking and prayer saved his life. His places of answered prayer are the sky and a field! His memories are fresh after nearly sixty years of flying.

> As a twenty-year-old recently discharged naval aviation cadet, I sat in the rear seat of a war surplus Stearman Trainer. The lowering cloud base deposited a light misty rain on my goggles. The occasional automobile, which I could make out below, was using its headlights, and the sparse cockpit instruments became visible due to their phosphorescent paint. I was startled to see that the exhaust was visible as a bright blue torch as it poured from the collector ring.
>
> I wanted to be logical, but the airfield to which I was returning had no lights, and I could fly right over it and not see it. The plane had no battery, so no lights or radio, and I felt it was a hazard. Since I was over open country, I considered bailing out. It's an old cliché that flying an airplane can be hours of boredom, interspersed with a few seconds of sheer terror. This is where the terror set in. The passage of years never dims the feelings I had as I slapped my left breast for the reassurance that the chute harness would give. After several slaps and a frantic search for the D-ring, I remembered that it was only a couple of cushions I was sitting on. The chutes were out for repacking.
>
> The situation was hopeless. The airplane was trimmed okay, so I turned it loose and let it do the flying. I had a clear vision of a tombstone with my name on it.
>
> I finally began to pray. I acknowledged to God that this was all my own doing, and I didn't want to harm anyone else. I asked for help and promised better

efforts if I somehow survived. I became calmer and relaxed. When I regained the controls, the airplane seemed heavier.

A lighted water tower came into view. Then I saw a uniform black area to my right, so I said, "Let's get this over with," and I pulled the engine to idle and set up a glide. At this point the unmistakable Georgia drawl of my former instructor sounded in my ears, "You don't go blunderin' into no strange field without lookin' it over first—when you got a good engine!" I advanced the throttle and avoided some tall trees that seemed to be along a ditch. There was some kind of mound near the house that might be a haystack, and maybe this uniform area was a hay field. I set up for a landing toward the hoped-for haystack. I turned off the gas at the end of a downwind and entered a side-slip to a landing. When I sensed the time was ripe I braked sequentially, and as the plane slowed, the engine began to sputter. After braking to a stop, I turned the gas back on and taxied past what *was* a haystack. I went through all of the shutdown rituals and locked the controls. I felt giddy as I stood on the cushions, walked onto the left wing, and fell into a heap near the fuselage.

I'd heard the voice of my instructor, but the front cockpit was really empty! I thanked God for what he had done. The odds against pulling off something like this were astronomical. I felt there must be something I was supposed to do with my life. I *do* know that in college, where it was fashionable to be an agnostic, I had no trouble staying *out* of fashion, and may have even had an effect on some who were teetering.

On the few occasions when I have found myself in the backseat of one of those old biplanes, all of the sensations of that night come rushing back.

In Bill's case, a crisis afforded him the opportunity to tell about God's goodness!

Still other places become signs of assurance. My friend Tom H. writes about two sacred places, one about which I quoted in an earlier chapter, and the other that is a place of hope.

> I thought of two rather odd sacred places. First, my kitchen. Here, I prepare meals for my family; thus it is here that I express my love for my family. It is also where I experience God's love and the wonders of the bounty God has provided for us.
>
> Second, my wife, Patti, and I visited the office of a radiation oncologist. Patti had been diagnosed with cancer; she had been treated with chemotherapy. The medical professionals decided that she also needed radiation therapy. The radiation oncologist offered us compassion and hope that only a believer in a compassionate and loving God could offer. The doctor's office will always be a sacred place for me.
>
> I realize that these two places are rather mundane, but I am a firm believer in a God who reveals divinity in the ordinary. For God, miracles are an easy way of getting our attention. The ordinary requires God to take a chance.

Patti died a few months later. Tom and their son acknowledge the many ways God helped all three of them during and after Patti's illness.

god's promise

The prophet Jeremiah acquired a place that we might call a field of hope.[7] God took a big chance with such an ordinary, foolish location.

Read Jeremiah 32. The Chaldean (Babylonian) army besieged Jerusalem, while Jeremiah himself was imprisoned at the palace of Judah under orders from King Zedekiah. Why did Zedekiah imprison him? Jeremiah had spoken treasonous words: the Chaldeans would capture Jerusalem and take the king to Babylon.

This is the situation. The days of the kingdom of Judah were drawing to a close; in the year 587 BCE, the prophet's prediction would take place. But before that, and while Jeremiah was confined, the Lord told him that his cousin Hanamel would shortly arrive to sell him a field at Anathoth, which was Jeremiah's hometown (32:7). Hanamel indeed arrived at the royal court, so Jeremiah "knew that this was the word of the LORD" (v. 8). He shortly purchased the field for seventeen shekels of silver. The text doesn't elaborate how this transaction occurred while Jeremiah was imprisoned, but the text does describe the business transaction in great detail (vv. 9-15).

Jeremiah addressed the Lord with a long prayer (vv. 17-25). "Nothing is too hard for you," he prayed (v. 17). The Lord is a faithful God who showed mighty power to Israel and gave them the land. But God also brought judgment upon God's people; Jerusalem was about to fall; exile was not far off. Yet God instructed Jeremiah to purchase a field!

God responded: yes, the city was about to fall because of the people's sins (vv. 26-35). Yet God would gather them and return them to the land. Exile would not last forever; "Just as I have brought all this great disaster upon this people, so I will bring upon them all the good fortune that I now promise them. . . . Fields shall be bought for money, and deeds shall be signed and sealed and witnessed. . . . For I will restore their fortunes, says the LORD" (vv. 42, 44).

Contrast Jeremiah's field of hope with a place of no hope. Let's back up a few chapters to Jeremiah 26 which describes events from about 609 BCE. In a sermon to worshipers in the Temple, Jeremiah scratched a very raw wound.

> Thus says the LORD: Stand in the court of the LORD's house, and speak to all the cities of Judah that come to worship in the house of the LORD. . . . You shall say to them: Thus says the LORD: If you will not listen to me, to walk in my law that I have set before you, and to heed the words of my servants the prophets whom I send to you

> urgently—though you have not heeded—then I will make this house like Shiloh, and I will make this city a curse for all the nations of the earth.
>
> The priests and the prophets and all the people heard Jeremiah speaking these words in the house of the LORD. . . . then [they] laid hold of him, saying, "You shall die! Why have you prophesied in the name of the LORD, saying, 'This house shall be like Shiloh'?" (Jeremiah 26:2, 4-9)

Jeremiah's entire sermon is recorded in chapter 7. There God warned the people, "If you truly amend your ways and your doings, if you truly act justly one with another, if you do not oppress the alien, the orphan, and the widow, or shed innocent blood in this place, and if you do not go after other gods to your own hurt, then I will dwell with you in this place, in the land that I gave of old to your ancestors forever and ever" (7:5-7). But the people cannot count on God's dwelling if they continue doing wrong: "Has this house, which is called by my name, become a den of robbers in your sight? . . . Go now to my place that was in Shiloh, where I made my name dwell at first, and see what I did to it for the wickedness of my people Israel" (vv. 11-12).

Part of that verse is familiar because of Jesus' similarly inflammatory usage. After Jeremiah said these things, the people wanted to kill him. Why was Shiloh such an emotional subject?

The biblical city of Shiloh remains mysterious because of a dearth of information. Probably located at the present town of Seilun, Shiloh is first mentioned in Joshua, and then in Judges and 1 Samuel, as the center of worship, where the Tabernacle was erected.[8] The ark was kept at the holy place of Shiloh, priests made sacrifices there, and the Israelite leaders guided the people from that place. Certainly the Lord was present there.

But Shiloh dropped from the story. What happened? First Samuel 4:21 states only that the glory of God had departed Israel because the

Philistines had captured the ark of God (see Ps. 78:60-61). Did the Philistines destroy the city (see Ps. 78:62-64)? Was it abandoned? Archaeological evidence is inconclusive as to the town's destruction.[9] In time Israelite government and worship shifted to Jerusalem. One of my seminary professors offered an interesting suggestion: the memory of Shiloh's loss was too painful for even Scripture to record.

On one level we understand Jeremiah's point: any human institution is finite and will pass away. But our faith needs certain anchors. If I lost my most important places, I'd have a very difficult time. God would seem distant. If you implied that God was punishing me, I'd be angry at you.

We should never presume to know God's purposes in someone else's life, especially regarding God's judgment. True, we bring many adverse situations upon ourselves through our carelessness, wrongdoing, and fallibility. We're also struck down by circumstances beyond our control. But if someone tells you that God is punishing you because of a crisis, that person is wrong! Jeremiah's preaching was empowered by God's Spirit for a special time and situation.

I focus on Shiloh because it symbolizes pain and grief, the awful disappointment when God's promises seem to break down, the terrible absence that drives us to God. But God does not leave us hopeless. Thus the story of Jeremiah's field. Who would purchase land when the nation is about to fall? By the world's standards, only a fool. But a simple field becomes a sign of the hope of the future, God's hope. Jerusalem does not become Shiloh; in the days of Ezra and Nehemiah the Temple is rebuilt and God's people are reestablished. God's promises are eternal.

You're in a terrible situation. Then, something strange happens. Water appears in view where you hadn't noticed. A grave becomes a place of hope for the future. Unexpected peace comes as you seek help for your loved one. A hill and creek become places of healing. A simple field becomes a sign of hope for the future—God's wide place of hope within a world filled with sadness and unanswered questions.

exercises

1. In your notebook name a place in your life that strengthens your faith when times are tough. Discuss which qualities of that place make it a reminder of God's love. Visualize that place when you're feeling troubled. If you're artistic, paint a picture or take a photograph of the place. Keep the tangible image close by; for instance, use the photograph as a bookmark in your Bible.

2. Look through photographs of friends or family members whom you miss. Live in the memories for a while. Realize that God exists in the past, present, and future altogether! Imagine God accompanying you on a trip back to a place where you experienced a painful time (or for that matter, a happy time you now miss).

3. Name the most painful places of your life. What happened there? Also name your own Massahs and Meribahs: places where you struggled with anxiety and questions. Such places may overlap with the others. Imagine God asking you to explain honestly how you feel about that place. Write your explanation in your notebook in the form of a letter, addressing God. If you're angry at God, write that down too. Consider burning or burying your letter as a sign of your trust that God will take care of you.

4. Write down strategies for calming yourself when you feel trapped in a place. Does prayer help? (Sometimes prayer is frantic!) How are your prayers answered when you feel desperate?

5. Read again Psalm 139, especially verses 11-12. Imagine God's light breaking through clouds. Let that light shine upon old hurts and anxieties that you still carry. Don't do anything; just let your mind wander as you imagine God's brightness.

5 church places

My mother's side of the family is filled with churchgoers. A year after my great-great-great-grandparents arrived at Four Mile, they helped found the prairie's first church. My distant cousin, C. C. Crawford, was a Christian Church minister and theologian, while a great-great-great-uncle, Ben Mahon, was a locally renowned "hard-shell Baptist" preacher of the late 1800s.

Theological discussions abounded at family get-togethers. So did politics—the two subjects that, Mom cautioned me, should be handled with care for people's feelings. Some of my relatives disliked the Methodist Church, I suppose because Methodists baptize babies, who are not conscious of sin and therefore have no need of the repentance that precedes adult immersion baptism. But our forebearers, my Crawford great-grandparents, were active in the former Methodist Episcopal Church. My pastor, Jim, puts it this way: thanks to faithful predecessors, Jesus gets into our genealogy.

Grandma Grace had a friend, Hubert Griffith,

who had achieved fifty years of perfect Sunday school attendance at the Brownstown, Illinois, Christian Church. I thought that was cool and hoped to set my own record. In ten years I missed Sunday school only because of illness. Even on vacations, Mom and I visited churches. We had a great time. I report this not out of a false sense of spiritual accomplishment but because the experience was so positive, especially since we visited churches outside our own denomination. Mom and I were ecumenical without knowing the word. (Dad sat in the car, reading Westerns.) Today my mind goes back to Sunday school rooms in now-forgotten towns in Missouri, Colorado, and Wyoming; rooms where I breezed in for an hour, shared the lesson with kids my age (where are they now?), and then went on my way. Every Sunday school we visited was warm and friendly.

By the time I was eighteen, my mother and I began attending the First United Methodist Church in Vandalia. The building, one of those lovely old turn-of-the-century churches common in small towns, sits two blocks north of downtown. My father had several friends who attended that church, so when my mother and I attended so did he—the first time in my life all three of us had gone to church together.

I was a freshman at a nearby Christian college, and my early, largely unconscious appreciation of church, theology, and spirituality came to fruition. Over the next few years the pastor helped me explore pastoral ministry and smoothed my way to divinity school. He helped me find copies of books like *The Interpreter's Bible* series and Karl Barth's *Church Dogmatics*, the latter of which I used in my doctoral work. My dad, who hadn't attended church since his childhood, joined the church. I taught Sunday school—not very well but I gave it my best. I did better giving "Bicentennial Minute" talks about local history during church services in 1976. My mother and father enjoyed social occasions at the church. When a church group began a ministry to people with disabilities, called Evergreen Outreach, Dad, using his automotive expertise, helped them select the best type of van. It was a happy time for me and my parents!

My association with the church didn't end, of course. Beth and I married in that chapel in 1984. When Dad died in 1999, his funeral was held at that church. I wept not only because of my loss but in gratitude for that church and the wonderful congregation.

most important places

When I discuss "church" and "church places" in this chapter, I don't mean a place with particular architectural and aesthetic characteristics, although that would be a correct usage. I mean the assembly of people who meet in a specific place, who worship and serve together and share a history. We may be strongly attracted or repelled by a church building but we've only scratched the surface of what that place is like.

Church is, potentially at least, your most important place. If all goes well, in churches we can find answers to our questions, a sense of peace, of wholeness and balance. Churches point us to the reality of God, God with us, God reconciled with us. The ethicist Stanley Hauerwas has provocatively argued that church, rather than family, is the most important place for the shaping of our character. "The love that we have toward our spouses and our children follows, rather than determines, the kind of love that we learn in the church through our being a people pledged to be faithful to God's call."[1] Our character is shaped by our relationship to God's faithfulness, and in turn by the community of people likewise seeking to grow in God's Spirit. Love, writes Hauerwas, is not "some affection for another that contributes to my own sense of well-being" but "the steady gaze on another that does not withdraw regard simply because they fail to please." That love "is first learned through being required to love our brothers and sisters who, like us, are pledged to be disciples of Christ."[2]

My friend Diana tells of the time she and her husband were temporarily separated:

> During that time, my husband accepted the Lord as his Savior. He began attending a small church in northern

> Arkansas. They loved him and supported him for the next six months while I was in Illinois.
>
> When I returned, we bought a house. We had nothing and the house was in shambles. This church came to the house, hauled off trash, cleaned, painted, and then made sure we had it furnished with all the furniture and fixtures we needed before they left. I don't think I've ever felt so much love, especially from people who barely knew me.
>
> Love is what a church is all about. Jesus is love, so if we are his children we must also love others. This church had a great pastor, great music, great teaching and fellowship, but *love* is what made this church.

Chances are if you have a church that's truly a wide place, it's the sort of church that Diana describes!

what kind of place is your church?

Trying to describe favorite "church places" is like trying to describe favorite "outdoor places." The variety and possibilities are vast. If you're a churchgoer, think about your own church place. At the risk of making your brain hurt, let me provide several questions (in no particular order) to guide you in understanding what kind of place your church is.[3]

Is this a prayerful and praying church? Does a prayer chain network support the members and the community? Does the church have classes and ministries for a range of age groups? If your church has families with babies, is there a well-staffed nursery?

Is your church ethnically homogeneous or heterogeneous? How about socioeconomically? Do women and men share leadership roles?

Are worship services engaging and meaningful? Do you look forward to worship and come away energized? What various styles of music are used? Do sermons emphasize not only conversion but also the importance of Christ's ongoing power to transform us?

Has volunteerism been wonderful or painful in this congregation in the past? What is the level of interest in mission and outreach? Do people feel fulfilled in their volunteer/service roles?

What kind of human nature is revealed at this church? Are people in this congregation thoughtful? Do they love? Are they responsive to people in crisis? Do they transcend their own socioeconomic status in order to care for those of a different life situation? Do they affirm one another's human fallibility?

Is there a climate of good communication in your church? Who speaks the most at board/council meetings? Are they positive, can-do people? Do they respect the pastor and staff? Do they work well with others? Is voting on issues helpful for this congregation? Are meetings brief and meaningful?

Is this church growing, declining, or plateaued in numerical membership? Is it a country church; an old downtown church; a suburban church; a small, or medium, or large church?

Is the pastor a good fit for the church? Does his or her leadership style support the church? What is the congregation's theological outlook and vision? What is the pastor's theological outlook and vision? What are the church's theological "nonnegotiables" (if any)?

How well have staff succeeded at the church before? What kinds of pastors and staff has the church had? Does the congregation respond to pastoral leadership? Is the pastor aware of the feelings of the people?

Who are the congregation's best leaders? Are they being used in the church in the most effective way? Who are the opinion shapers within the congregation?

Where do the church's ideas come from? Do they come from the people, empowered to do ministry? Do they come from the pastor's vision for the church? If from the pastor, are the ideas commensurate with the realities of the congregation? If from the people, do the ideas reflect a commitment and vision? Are innovative ideas embraced?

What is the church's history? What are the church's most important traditions, its happiest moments, and its most painful events? What have been some aspects of the church's recent history? What are the points of resistance and dissatisfaction in the congregation? What seems to bring out the best in the congregation? How has change been handled in the past? How can "the serenity prayer" be applicable to this congregation (that is, what can be changed, what cannot be, and who is wise enough to know the difference)?

Where does the congregation want to be in X years? What are its goals? Does the congregation think in those terms? Will the congregation balk at a pastor who will help the congregation to work toward those goals? What is the congregation's current financial situation?

If the church relates to a denominational structure, what is the quality of that relationship?

If you think about the various aspects of your church, you start to see what a rich, multifaceted, "deep" kind of place it is! Many factors create a pastiche of grace and humanness.

church homes

As a personal preference, I'm sentimental for small- to medium-sized churches, five hundred in membership or less, I also love churches with old woodwork and historic stained glass. Many people find large churches meaningful, but you're mistaken if you think a particular church style or size is "ideal," because the Spirit is free to work as it wills, where it wills! Paul scarcely mentioned numerical growth in his letters; he was more concerned with ensuring his churches were faithful to God's Spirit.

From Paul we get the venerable image of the church as "the body of Christ" (Eph. 4:12-13; Rom. 12:5). Whenever my head hurts from sinus pain, my whole body stalls. My feet work fine, but they alone can't keep me upright; I need the balance provided by my inner ears. So it is with churches. Each congregation is made up of different aspects: "subsystems" and small congregations like choirs, singles groups, seniors groups, Sunday school and weekday classes, committees, volunteer groups, and so on. The health of the church body depends upon the proper function of all the parts, which work together. The Sunday school program may be healthy, but if the choir is threatening to mutiny, the whole church suffers. A single gossip or self-assertive person can hurt the entire congregation.[4]

When churches function well, people live by faith in Jesus and walk by the Spirit (Gal. 2:20; 5:16-26). People love one another and live in harmony (Rom. 13:8-14; 15:1, 5). People are not conceited and envious of each other (Gal. 5:26); if they compete, it is to show honor (Rom. 12:10). People do not gossip, pass judgment, and find fault when someone errs or strays, but instead lead the person back to the right path through gentleness and self-awareness (Rom. 14:13; Gal. 6:1-2). They bear one another's failings (Rom. 15:1). They are more concerned with their own faithfulness than picking at the work of others, knowing they too can fall into temptation (Gal. 6:4-5). They seek not to become stumbling blocks to others (1 Cor. 8:13).

Churches are human, frail places. We bring our whole selves to Christ: "Just as I am, without one plea," goes that beloved hymn. But when we bring our whole selves to Christ, we bring our best and worst selves, not always recognizing the difference. Difficult as it is, we should try to approach church life with a realistic perspective combined with a healthy sense of humor at ourselves and human foibles.

While working on another book project, I read a wonderful text called *Discover Your Spiritual Type: A Guide to Individual and Congregational Growth* by Corinne Ware.[5] Ware notes that we all approach spirituality in different, though perhaps overlapping, ways. Some people enjoy a more emotional kind of worship (music, praise choruses, testimony), while other people like a more orderly, intellectual, and liturgical worship. Still others "find God" best in social action and causes, while others appreciate meditation, intuition, silent contemplation, and so on. Given human nature, we think that what works for us should work for everyone, so too many churches emphasize a certain type of worship or educational program and then expect everyone to fall in line. But as all of us learn in different ways and at different paces, we also learn about and worship God in different ways.

When we find a church home, we feel comfortable because the style and fellowship of a congregation fit us. We feel wanted, needed, and missed when we're gone. We find friendships—one of the defining things about church (John 15:14-15), because friends listen, support, and encourage us to grow.

When childhood churches were nurturing and helpful, those congregations continue to brighten and bless our days. Mary, a cousin of mine, writes:

> Although my mom's family was Presbyterian, we were Methodists because the church was right across the street from our house, in our little town of seventy-five people. So much for dogma; proximity ruled! The church was my safe haven. I helped my grandma, who prepared the bread and grape juice for Communion, although I partook of a lot of the Communion supplies while helping. I did church, Sunday school, MYF, choir, and so forth. The day my mom called to tell me the church was being closed because of small attendance and insufficient contributions was one of the saddest days of my life. (By then I had lived elsewhere for many years.) When she helped clean out the church she saved a red Christmas decoration from the church Christmas tree. It's still my favorite Christmas decoration and it goes on our tree each year.

Church homes support us when we're most in need. My friend Judy, retired Vandalia statehouse site superintendent, writes of her home church:

> I lost my mother to liver cancer in March 2003. She was buried on a Wednesday, and the following Friday I had colon cancer surgery in St. Louis. The surgery went well. I came home the following Friday. Saturday morning I

> became sick again and was taken by helicopter back to St. Louis. I was there two weeks and in a rehab center for another two weeks. I couldn't even walk. To this day they're not sure what happened: perhaps medication or stress.
>
> I'm called the "miracle woman." I was in God's hands; God truly blessed me. It is so nice for the medical doctors to agree. If this hadn't happened to me, our son would not have been checked for colon cancer. He did have a growth that can turn into colon cancer.
>
> Not only did my church's prayer chain work overtime, but church prayer chains all over Vandalia and also up in Ramsey, my hometown north of Vandalia.

When Judy needed help, her friends got to work and prayed diligently. Their prayers not only helped her but also, unexpectedly, her son too.

the pastor's place

Pastors need a special "sense of place" as they serve their parish. They also need to take time to get to know the congregation sufficiently well to make fair judgments about the church. This is not something that can, under many circumstances, be hurried. A pastor needs to know his or her people's stories, to listen effectively to them over an appropriate period of time. A pastor's style may even get in the way of effective listening. Getting to know a congregation in a patient, listening way is strong, loving leadership.

In the lingo of recent books, pastors lead best when they are "transformational" rather than "transactional." The latter has to do with management effectiveness, deploying volunteers, troubleshooting, an effective leadership style, and so on, while transformational leadership consists of the ability to inspire, motivate, and unite a group of people to attain goals and work for congregational change. The transformational leader unites people (who may not share the same ideas and values) in the fulfillment of shared goals. Such leadership requires strength in preaching and worship; the ability to identify, inspire, and work with leaders in the church; the ability to stay close to the people while not managing everything; the willingness to take risks and to take the initiative; and the endurance needed to work through congregational inertia, resistance, conflict, and poor internal communication. This is obviously more difficult than managerial leadership, although both types of leadership are necessary.[6]

As R. Paul Stevens and Phil Collins put it in *The Equipping Pastor*, leadership is "L=(L, F, S)," or "leadership equals the function of the leader, the followers, and the situation."[7] Although the pastor exhibits the kind of spiritual authority that gains people's confidence, the pastor really derives his or her leadership from the congregation. One way a good pastor becomes a good leader is to know that congregation deeply. Because a church place is such a complex collection of people, traditions, community issues, power issues, and the like, a good pastor tries to understand the culture and "system" of the congregation rather than imposing ill-fitting programs upon a congregation.[8]

> The Spirit wants to change us!

Change agency is a term for bringing about positive, effective change to a congregation in order for that congregation to minister effectively in its community. Change may include cultivating interdependence; identifying and addressing problems within the congregation; caring for "subsystems"; moving the people beyond mindless voluntarism; and bringing a sense of joy, fun, and Sabbath to a church. Change agency is difficult and requires the cooperation of the people as well as strength and patience on the part of the leader. (One author identifies no fewer than thirty-three hypotheses to account for resistance to change in an organization!) Change requires a deep appreciation of the congregation and must be conducted not by "management" but by spirit, positive reinforcement, passion, and compassion. Change is brought to a congregation slowly, sometimes indirectly, and through cultivation of the whole church climate. It requires time and cannot be rushed. Change is brought about when the pastor is close to the people and evaluates his or her spirituality and leadership within the context of the congregation.[9] For the pastor, church is truly a challenging, multifaceted kind of place.

the sine qua non

Jesus said that wherever two or three are gathered, he is in the midst of them (Matt. 18:20). He has established us securely in the presence of God (Ps. 102:28). Similarly, Paul calls our bodies temples of the Holy Spirit, so whenever we gather, God is present with us if we truly have the Spirit (1 Cor. 3:16). Wherever people who are led in the Spirit are gathered, that is a place where God is! Strictly speaking, it doesn't matter what kind of people we are; the Spirit's presence determines the sacredness of our gathering; it is essential, the sine qua non.

But remember: the Spirit wants to change us! As you read his letters, Paul stresses justification by faith and also living by the Spirit (Rom. 6:19, Gal. 5:16). The two cannot be separated; coming to Christ also means giving oneself over to the power of the Spirit. The Spirit provides us with things we need to grow in God's presence: "love, joy, peace, patience, kindness, generosity, faithfulness, gentleness, and self-control" (Gal. 5:22-23). But the Spirit also leads us to "crucify" the things that separate us from God: "fornication, impurity, licentiousness, idolatry, sorcery, enmities, strife, jealousy, anger, quarrels, dissensions, factions, envy, drunkenness, carousing, and things like these" (Gal. 5:19-21; see also Rom. 6:6). "If we live by the Spirit," says Paul, "let us also be guided by the Spirit" (Gal. 5:25).

For Paul, seeking God is also seeking the fruit of the Spirit (Gal. 5:22-25) and becoming new creations (2 Cor. 5:17).

Read Galatians: it's a short but important book. The Galatians

(Gentile Christians; Galatia was a province in central Asia Minor) had received God's Spirit. Why was that so momentous? Because God's Spirit—the same Spirit who had spoken through the prophets and raised Jesus Christ from the dead—had come to them and blessed them. The Spirit had come to them not because of anything they did to earn it but because of faith. Furthermore, the Spirit had come to persons of a different tradition than the Jews: the God of Abraham, Isaac, and Jacob had touched the lives of this group of non-Jews, and now they were children of God (Gal. 3:25-28).

Paul is frustrated because certain teachers at Galatia taught the necessity of circumcision for Christians (Gal. 5:2-6). The Galatians should have been happy with God's gift; but now they were trying to "add" something to God's unmerited faith.

We all do this. We try to add things to God's gifts. We think we need to perform religious rites in a certain way; to attend a particular spiritual retreat to be part of the "in" group; to convince God to love us if we do X. How many times have you prayed for a favor from God—adding that you'll change your behavior in some way in order to convince God to help you? This just doesn't work—because God loves us regardless of our merit. As Archbishop Desmond Tutu puts it, "There is nothing you can do that will make God love you less. There is nothing you can do to make God love you more. God's love for you is infinite, perfect, and eternal."[10] If we have the Spirit working in our lives, we've no need of "extra" spiritual things; God has already taken the initiative! But it's difficult for us to allow ourselves to be changed in potentially painful ways (Rom. 6:5-11), even though the outcome is better: life in Christ!

the sacrament is a place

The worship service provides many opportunities for God to create wide places.[11] In the reading of the Word, the sermon, and in the Spirit, who empowers both, God creates and nourishes faith (Rom.

10:14-17). Not only do we express our faith in music and singing (Col. 3:16; James 5:13), but we're taught by the music. Moments of prayer, silence, and reflection provide opportunities to connect with God. The liturgical seasons order our years around the stories and teachings of sacred Scripture. The fellowship of worship is not incidental, for Christ joins us when we gather (Matt. 18:20).

My wife, Beth, a teacher and university administrator, remembers her childhood church:

> Growing up in Lemont, Illinois, I associated churches with the town's sturdy structures erected from the quarried limestone that made way for the Illinois and Michigan canal. Immigrants from many European countries made their way to this little town, built the canal, founded congregations, and sustained their cultures in faith communities. Thus, there was the Polish Catholic Church, the German Catholic Church, the Lithuanian Catholic Church, the Italian Catholic Church, and so on. When I was in sixth grade, my parents responded to a door-to-door campaign by the Swedish Lutherans, and we joined the legions who now hear themselves in the stories of *A Prairie Home Companion*.
>
> We worshiped in Gothic style facing an altar decorated with dark brown spires, lit by golden candelabra, and flanked by chairs thronelike in their appearance. Ornate, richly hued stained glass filtered brilliant sunlight by day and cast forbidding shadows from streetlights by night. Darkly paneled staircases led from vestry and basement—secret passages known to the stewards of light and wine. Facing forward, we creaked into wooden pews and sang with pipe organ in response to the chanting of ancient liturgy. Sanctuary was found in the coolness and calm of tranquil moments of prayer. We stood at the reading of the Gospel and again when a hymn verse bespoke Holy Trinity. Liturgical colors swathed altar, lectern, and robes. A cycle of Sundays and seasons marked the passing of years with special worship

> occasions in midweek for Advent and Lent. I came of age in this historic place of devotion to God, family, community, and heritage.
>
> For me, the most sacred of memories in this yearly cycle is Easter Sunday morning following Good Friday. For Good Friday service, the church was emptied of all ornamentation: the candlesticks, vases, the altar paraments, and the cross: everything down to the bare wood. The pastor did not wear his alb and stole. Then on Sunday morning, the choir processed up from the basement, carrying each item to again fill the tomblike sanctuary with light and color and joy. Singing hallelujahs, we carried candles. Proclaiming "Christ the Lord is risen today," we lifted candlesticks. Rejoicing, we placed scriptures on the altar. And as happy Christians and Swedes alike—by birth or by adoption—we adorned altar rail, window well, and our winter weary souls with the bloom of a hundred Easter lilies.

The worship service is a place that draws us close to God!

Think about baptism and the Eucharist as places where God makes God's self known. They're actually important, powerful places, but you may not think of them that way at all.

Let's say I walk into your church and, in the name of Jesus Christ, heal your disease. Is that a "better" miracle than the grace of the Lord's Supper or the grace of baptism? Most of us would say yes, but we'd be wrong!

Dutch theologian G. C. Berkouwer notes that in biblical times God became known through miraculous signs. "As God's work progresses," he writes, "miraculous signs give place to sacraments. It is not a drop from riches to poverty, but a rise from a wealth of salvation to a greater wealth in the knowledge of faith and the unction of the Holy Spirit (1 John 2:20)."[12] In other words, although God still gives miraculous signs, God intends for the sacraments to be even greater signs of the Spirit's work among us! The sacraments are no cheap substitute for miracles but are richer than miracles, because through them the Spirit helps us live by faith rather than by proof. Because of the sacraments, we have a better help for our faith than did the first disciples. That people "yearn wistfully for special signs and new revelations" from God, says Berkouwer, is "a serious devaluation of Word and sacrament and of an emasculation of the power of faith."[13]

"Your life is hidden with Christ in God" (Col. 3:3). I remember feeling profoundly comforted by that verse as I sat in a lonely place, a desk deep in a campus library wing. Your real life, your real identity, is in Christ. How do you know that? Baptism is one way to understand that you are hidden in Christ. Baptism is a sign that God has reached down and claimed you, giving you life and grace. Baptism clothes you (Gal. 3:27). My friend Pastor Dick writes:

> Our baptism garments are intended more to identify us to ourselves than to others. They are often soiled, and it's easy to forget that we even have them. Why? Because they are transparent—just as we are transparent to God and just as it is best that we be transparent to one another.
>
> See-through garments are usually not recommended. The lifelong garment of baptism is the one exception. Consider that garment as you wear it today, humbly and faithfully.

When Martin Luther struggled with depression and anxiety, when he doubted God's love for him, he simply affirmed, "I am baptized."[14] Baptism is a sign of God's work.[15]

Churches baptize by various means and with different theological nuances and assumptions. God works powerfully among the unbaptized too; the thief on the cross, for instance, gained paradise, even though he had no baptism. Through we Christians will always differ on matters of doctrine and practice, we recognize that Christ is richly present for people with whom we may diverge significantly on theological issues such as baptism. God's love is always unmerited!

The Eucharist, along with baptism, is the sacrament that nearly all churches celebrate.[16] John Wesley, who founded the Methodist movement, liked to take Communion every four or five days; he considered the Eucharist an indispensable way by which the Holy Spirit is given to us. The Eucharist has several overlapping meanings. First, in sharing the cup and the bread, we share in the presence of Christ. We share together in God's grace. Second, we remember Christ's sufferings on our behalf. We recall how he chose the way of anguish, bloodshed, and death on behalf of our sins. The Eucharist helps our faith by reminding us of the basis of our faith (1 Cor. 11:23-26). Third, the Eucharist simultaneously reminds us of eternal life and prepares us for it. In sharing the elements, we receive the grace that saves and sanctifies us in preparation for heaven. The Eucharist is actually a harbinger of the afterlife. Fourth, the Eucharist is a sign and reminder that God loves us and works on our behalf.

thinking rightly about the sacraments

Pastors face two challenges regarding the sacraments. Once in a while, someone wants to be baptized again. That person, baptized previously, perhaps as an infant or young, uncomprehending adult, now understands the gospel and would like to receive baptism with full knowledge and repentance. Perhaps that person feels insecure about his or her faith and is not sure the first baptism "took." (I write from a United Methodist perspective; some denominations do require rebaptism.) Churches that practice infant baptism compound the problem by overemphasizing the "christening" aspect of the rite.

When such persons seek rebaptism, they're sincere in wanting to please God, but they may actually be devaluing God's grace in their lives. Baptism is God's own means of providing salvation, regardless of our understanding or merit. As we saw in Galatians, Paul is adamant that we have no signs of grace other than the Holy Spirit's own work.

The second challenge is the refusal of a few persons to share in the Eucharist. Paul famously stated, "Whoever, therefore, eats the bread or drinks the cup of the Lord in an unworthy manner will be answerable for the body and blood of the Lord. Examine yourselves, and only then eat of the bread and drink of the cup. For all who eat and drink without discerning the body, eat and drink judgment against themselves" (1 Cor. 11:27-29). Considering the context, the Corinthian worshipers were abusing the Lord's Supper. Dividing themselves into factions, probably along class lines, they did not share properly in the common meal, and while one person went hungry, another was well-fed and drunk (1 Cor. 11:17-22, 33-34). This is Paul's concern.

I knew at least one person who didn't commune because he did not want to "eat and drink judgment" upon himself. But Paul never said we must be worthy of the Lord's Supper! The Eucharist is the wide place where God accepts us with the love of a welcoming parent, regardless of what we've done or where we've been. In fact, the Eucharist is one of the most important places God has given us to know God! If it doesn't seem so, think about the Eucharist afresh, perhaps by studying the ceremony in your hymnal.

church and place

As Christians we are responsible for one another's Christian walk and well-being. Paul talks about "one body and one Spirit, . . . one hope of your calling, one Lord, one faith, one baptism, one God and Father of all" (Eph. 4:4-6). So when someone you know is in trouble, you're there for that person, praying, talking, listening, and helping. You "[bear] with one another in love," with "humility and gentleness, with patience" (Eph. 4:2).

Paul's letter to the Ephesians is remarkable; he wrote it in a very bad place, prison (3:1, 4:1, 6:20). But his captivity is not a matter of self-pity or distress (although suffering is involved). With Christ's help, Paul makes of his situation a positive metaphor. He is an "ambassador [for the gospel] in chains" (Eph. 6:20). As he is bound in prison, his congregation should live in "the bonds of peace" (4:3) by their faith in Christ, who has freed us from the captivity of sin and death in order to be "joined" as a common body. When Christians are joined together, they find strength rather than distress. They are stronger together, because they are together in Christ.

> We are responsible for one another's Christian walk and well-being.

It's easier to describe that kind of fellowship than actually to pull it off. I remember a *New Yorker* cartoon several years ago that depicted the Three Musketeers crossing their swords together. Instead of saying, "All for one and one for all," they declared together, "Every man for himself!" Too often we say, "One body in Christ," but don't mean it at all. What makes Paul's prison reflections so remarkable is that he isn't thinking primarily of his own drastic situation or how he's going to get himself out of this tight place. In his danger and isolation, he is instead thinking of the invisible bonds of love that are, in fact, far stronger than his chains.[17]

Love makes the church a wide place of grace.

exercises

1. Without necessarily doing extra research, write an informal history of your church. If you'd like, be creative and call it "The Ballad of My Church." What events are important to your church that might not get included in an "official" history (for instance, the day the pipes froze, the time So-and-So resigned from the board, and so on)?
2. Think about the worship service at your church. What part is the most spiritually helpful? The least? Are the sacraments meaningful to you or not? What would you say is the primary "means of grace" in your life right now?
3. Write down a description of the best church you've ever attended. The worst. What make those churches wonderful or terrible? Write a short story about those churches. How did God speak to you even in the difficult church?
4. Write a letter (but don't send it!) to a church person who, intentionally or not, caused you to "stumble." Express your feelings honestly but make your own healing your goal. Immediately destroy the letter to symbolize your forgiveness of that person and God's healing help.
5. Write a letter of appreciation to a pastor or Sunday school teacher who was especially influential for you. If that person is deceased or unavailable, write the letter anyway.

6 wide places of grace

My goal in this book has been to think about sacred places in our lives and how they become sites for Spirit and grace. I've not attempted to cover the range of special human places or to catalog all the special locations in the Bible. Instead, guided by stories both personal and biblical, I've invited you to reflect on how God moves in your life.

God creates "wide places," which is to say, God's grace works for our benefit, guiding, protecting, and instructing us. God gives us grace in our homes. God provides us places—both in childhood and adulthood—that are happy, safe, and peaceful. God reveals God's self in the splendor of nature, in the carefree locations of childhood. God touches our lives in difficult places, one time converting us, another time saving us from trouble, another time giving us peace and strength. God gives us places of Christian fellowship that help us grow in grace. God helps us when, on occasion, that fellowship breaks down.

Places illustrate ways that God both deals with us and helps us; places are both parable and memory.

> Places are both parable and memory.

Remember how Jacob honored God? He took the stone on which he had slept, anointed it, and called the place Bethel ("House of God"). The place became a visible reminder of God's faithfulness.

Remember that Hagar named her special place Beer-lahai-roi, which means something like "the well of one who sees and lives." The place reminded people that God sees and responds to people who are in need.

Remember that Abraham planted a tamarisk tree at the place called Beer-sheba, or "well of the oath." The place became a sign of the covenant made between him and Abimelech.

When tested by God, Abraham named another place, YHWH Jireh, or "the LORD will provide."

We studied several other places—Jeremiah's field, the burning bush, the road to Emmaus—which became symbols of God's faithfulness. There are other biblical examples too. A notable story comes from Joshua as the Israelites finally cross into the land.

> When the entire nation had finished crossing over the Jordan, the LORD said to Joshua: "Select twelve men from the people, one from each tribe, and command them, 'Take twelve stones from here out of the middle of the Jordan, from the place where the priests' feet stood, carry them over with you, and lay them down in the place where you camp tonight.'" Then Joshua summoned the twelve men from the Israelites, whom he had appointed, one from each tribe. Joshua said to them, "Pass on before the ark of the LORD your God into the middle of the Jordan, and each of you take up a stone on his shoulder, one for each of the tribes of the Israelites, so that this may be a sign among you. When

> your children ask in time to come, 'What do those stones mean to you?' then you shall tell them that the waters of the Jordan were cut off in front of the ark of the covenant of the LORD. When it crossed over the Jordan, the waters of the Jordan were cut off. So these stones shall be to the Israelites a memorial forever." (Joshua 4:1-7)

A pile of river rocks became a perpetual announcement that God creates amazing circumstances for God's people.

So did the Ebenezer. The second verse of the hymn "Come, Thou Fount of Every Blessing" begins, "Here I raise mine Ebenezer; Hither by Thy help I'm come." When I was a little boy, I hadn't a clue what that meant! I thought an Ebenezer was a drink that you raised as a Christmas toast (drawing from the obvious Charles Dickens connotations), though I dared not suggest such a thing to my nondrinking parents.

Now I know. The name signified yet another biblical place: a memorial stone to God. The story is found in 1 Samuel 7:12. Samuel erected the stone following a victory over the Philistines at Mizpah. "Ebenezer" means "stone of help," because Samuel said, "Thus far the LORD has helped us."

I love the humanness of that statement: God has been gracious so far. Will God be gracious again? Will we have faith enough to see? Or will God grow strangely silent? A special place needs to be set aside so we can remember—and if circumstances grow difficult, we can look back in reassurance.

The Bible gives us plenty of precedent for needing reassurance in our faith. When the psalmist couldn't find God, he remembered God's works.

> I will call to mind the deeds of the LORD;
> I will remember your wonders of old.
> I will mediate on all your work,
> and muse on your mighty deeds. (Psalm 77:11-12)

Even my favorite psalm, 121, begins with a question that can either be rhetorical or reassuring.

> I lift up my eyes to the hills—
> from where will my help come?
> My help comes from the LORD,
> who made heaven and earth. (Psalm 121:1-2)

The psalmist was not simply beholding scenery; he needed assistance for a steep terrain. The psalmist may have been journeying to Jerusalem, which is higher in elevation than other areas of Canaan. Who would keep him from stumbling along the hilly path? Does God—the maker of heaven and earth, the Lord of Israel—have sufficient power to keep the psalmist from falling? Of course. Not only that, but God has the power to protect the poet from other hazards (vv. 5-8). Yet God may seem unresponsive and absent, so the psalmist needs to reaffirm his own faith in God.

Consider your own special places as sites of God's grace. As you reflect upon those places, tell other people about your stories. Like Jacob's Bethel-stone, Joshua's river stones, and Samuel's stone of help, your sacred places testify to others!

spiritual disciplines

Earlier I talked about spirituality, a popular topic these days. Christian spirituality includes spiritual disciplines, which in turn aim at growth in the image of Christ. Spirituality is not merely the quest for peace of mind (although it can include that) but also means opening ourselves to the gifts of the Spirit, which change, prune, heal, and mature us. Dallas Willard identifies several spiritual disciplines that can help us on our faith journeys.[1] Several are called disciplines of *abstinence* because they entail sacrifice:

- *Solitude*: we take time in private for God, both to draw closer to God as well as to test our resiliency in aloneness.

- *Silence*: we avoid distracting noises and sounds as we pray, think, and read spiritually.
- *Fasting*: we voluntarily abstain from food for a time, with approval from a physician.
- *Frugality*: we discipline our spending to better serve God and others in need.
- *Chastity*: we discipline our sexuality, definitely one of our most stubborn drives!
- *Secrecy*: we refrain from telling others about our spiritual disciplines.
- *Sacrifice*: we strive to be more giving and frugal in order to depend on God for our needs.

There are also disciplines of *engagement*:

- *Study*: we read and reflect on God's Word.
- *Worship*: we open ourselves to God through songs and liturgy.
- *Celebration*: we're happy in our faith!
- *Service*: we use our time, talents, and means to help others.
- *Prayer*: we communicate with God.
- *Fellowship*: we do several of these other disciplines with other people.
- *Confession*: we share ourselves with those we trust in our fellowship.
- *Submission*: we're humble in a Christlike way.

Willard notes that practicing some of these disciplines (but probably not all of them at once) helps us grow in grace. These are not ways to earn grace but to mature in our relationship with God.

I briefly played on a Little League team years ago. I think my team was called the Browns, and if I remember right, we won two games in two years! Whenever I go walking near my mother's home, I walk down Locust Street, a pretty, lightly trafficked street, bordered by a series of parks and the ball field. For many boys and girls, such a field holds happy memories, but I wasn't good at sports. Eventually I realized the obvious: I was no athlete! More importantly, I had little desire to develop my meager abilities. Today, as I walk my childhood locations, that ball field reminds me of my lack of athletic discipline.

My friend Stacey, on the other hand, is a talented ice-skater who has competed nationally. She works out two hours a day, teaches skating, and also choreographs, usually by listening to music. She has natural gifts, but she also trains and hones her skills while teaching others to perform well and love the sport.

Think of spiritual disciplines as similar to physical discipline. Certainly Paul does in an easily misunderstood passage, 1 Corinthians 9:24-27. Being a sensitive witness to Christ may not come easily; love, compassion, and character must be developed. So the purpose of spiritual discipline, Paul says, is to ready us for effective outreach to others. Lest Paul be disqualified from the "race" of faith, he disciplines himself so he can be Christlike as "naturally" as an athlete can compete.

You can also think of spiritual discipline as a way to maintain a healthy relationship with God. Beth and I have been married for more than twenty years and have been friends for more than thirty years. Yet if one of us neglected the relationship—never talking, rarely coming home, squandering money, and so on—the legal marital relationship would remain for a while, but the quality of the relationship would be pretty poor, and the foundation would crumble fast!

> Sometimes answered prayer comes at us sideways.

So it is with our relationship to God. God is faithful and has done everything for us that we need to know and grow in God. Yet we have plenty of impediments to mature faith, including fear, mixed motives, stubbornness, and an inability to see the future. The Bible itself indicates that God can seem silent and distant at times. People faithful to their relationship with God have times of doubt, trouble, and anxiety, as we've seen from the Bible psalms and stories—so much more for those of us whose prayer life, fellowship time, charitable giving, Bible reading, and so on are "catch as catch can." Meaningful spiritual discipline helps us grow and remain open to God's Spirit.

Not only that, but spiritual discipline helps us become more closely attuned to God's will. Hard as it is to believe, God's purposes do not revolve around you and me alone. God is not bound by our expectations. Faithfulness on our part does not "leverage" God to act according to our dreams and desires. Answered prayer takes many forms; to paraphrase a popular saying, sometimes answered prayer comes at us sideways. Unless we dwell in God's presence regularly, we might miss God's goodness and guidance.

I'd like to modestly propose making "place" a complementary component of the practice of spiritual discipline. I'll explore some possible ways in the exercises that follow this chapter. But if we consider God as our "dwelling place" (Deut. 33:27, RSV note), our all-encompassing place (Ps. 24:1), then we begin to see God in all the places we are and will be. We begin to see God's sanctity in the places we live and the people we meet. Our sacred, special places become like Bethel, Beer-lahai-roi, YHWH Jireh, Ebenezer, Jeremiah's field, the road to Emmaus—signs and reminders of divine love.

he came to us

Throughout this study, I've shared some "sense of place" stories from several of my friends who live around the country. They generously wrote about locations sacred to them. My friend Duane, a university professor in education, writes about Jesus and place. I'll let Duane have the last word.

> Jesus was neither a tourist nor a traveler. But he did live in particular cities, on streets and in houses; he shopped among marketplaces and worshiped in simple synagogues. Jesus thoroughly lived "in place," becoming part of the

culture of those places yet elevating those cultures by his presence. Every secular place was made sacred by his presence. Jesus obliterated the false dichotomies of good or bad place, better or worse, sacred or secular, holy or sinful. He even tore down the notion of here and there. He was in all, from all, for all, God of Place and God in Place and God from Place.

Recently a group of leaders shared places they had encountered God and gotten in touch with their spiritual selves. Some spoke of finding God beside calm lakes, at special retreats in monasteries, or under the starry night on a European backpacking trip. When it came time for me to share, I had many places running through my mind. I grew up in California. I recalled driving through the thick forests of the redwoods. I remember backpacking in the desolate but majestic Trinity Forests. I remember lying in a grove of mighty sequoias, thinking about the reality that these trees had existed for millennia, even before Christ was born. I was even tempted to say that my favorite place was near Tuolumne meadows in Yosemite. Who could imagine a meadow at nine thousand feet! But more than the shores of the great Pacific or the silent beauty of Death Valley, a different place came to mind, when I was stunned by God's presence while visiting the men's bathroom at an outlet shopping center!

Many times since then, I have been stunned by the God who comes to odd places. This is the God worth knowing, who comes to me in my mundaneness.

We should not be amazed that God would be with us in the beauty of God's creation. What is unexpected, and in keeping with the Jesus of the Bible, is that God would be with me in whatever place I went. I was liberated from the God of special place, the God of monks and monasteries, of spiritual buildings and sacred campuses. Now, I saw a God who would be with the mental patients in the psych wards, a God of the drunk, on the ground outside the pub. God could be anyplace, because God's presence made it a temple. Because God is passionate about each of us, he assumed our place, that we might be elevated to his. God could be in place, at home, with the painful and hurting in the hospital and with the bored and boring.

In short, the message of Christianity is that Jesus is in Place, at home with where we are. This is the ultimate liberation from all pretension of there being more or less sacredness to places. It is an invitation to go into all the world, into every place, and know that God is with us. This message reaffirms a different deity than that which is promoted by many in this world. We need not come up to the mountain to find God. God has come down to find us, to linger with us. God comes to eat with us, where we are (Rev. 3:20). God lingers wherever we find ourselves, whether it is gazing up at sequoias or fretfully poring over our monthly bills.

For many, this is a wild claim. It challenges the view that churches are more sacred than public schools, or that God's wisdom is more prevalent in universities than in mental wards. It challenges the notion that there is more freedom to be found by a vacationer on a cruise ship than by a death row inmate in a cold prison. No. Jesus has been to all these places. His presence makes each a place where we can encounter God. The Citizen of all places uses that right to be our companion where we are. Jesus has obliterated the harsh lines of distinction between all places by coming to all of us, where we exist. God is surely with us. Wherever we are, God will meet us there! That is good news! Finally, a God who doesn't need us to trek up a mountain to find God.

God came to us.

exercises

Chapter 6 lists several traditional spiritual disciplines drawn from Dallas Willard's *The Spirit of the Disciplines: Understanding How God Changes Lives*. For these last exercises, put these disciplines "in place," so to speak. Take a few minutes with each, but don't hurry the process; take the time you need.

1. Disciplines of abstinence:
   - *Solitude*: When you take time to be private for God, where do you go? Think about a good place where you won't be disturbed and can stay open to God's guidance.
   - *Silence*: Similarly, what is a good quiet place where you can communicate with God? Be aware that silence and solitude can be troubling. When our bodies are at ease, our minds can fixate on problems and old wounds; disturbing thoughts intrude on our devotion. Give those things to God too. Ask God for help in dealing with those things according to his best judgment.
   - *Fasting*: If your doctor says it's okay, try fasting. Skip lunch, for instance, or have a light meal in the early morning then fast until nightfall. You'll feel hungry, of course, but let that hunger remind you of God's blessings and also the physical needs of people. As you go about your daily routine in places, think about people who are hurting because of deprivation. Think about ways you might help those in need.
   - *Frugality*: Where do you shop? Are you attentive to God when you're shopping? (Probably not.) Think about your favorite shopping areas and consider how you can use your money wisely and sacrificially.
   - *Chastity*: This is another personal one! Think about places where you've expressed your sexuality—including places that you're ashamed of. Think about people you may be

attracted to in an inappropriate way. Give all these thoughts and places to God (who knows them already, after all) and ask God for clarity and guidance in your sexual needs.

- *Secrecy*: This means that, when you're doing spiritual disciplines, you don't tell anyone! Ask God to help you communicate your spirituality to others in ways other than telling them you're fasting, meditating, and so on. "Let your gentleness be known to everyone" (Phil. 4:5).
- *Sacrifice*: Are there any needs or desires you can't quite surrender to God? Do you think you can trust God completely? This is another tough discipline! As you undertake other disciplines in your everyday places, ask God to help you rely upon God's help in a mature, trusting way.

2. Disciplines of engagement:
   - *Study*: Where do you read the Bible and good books? Find a place where reading feels natural. In the case of Bible study, if necessary, place multiple copies of the Bible around your house to remind you to read as you break from daily tasks.
   - *Worship*: Read chapter 5 and think about your own church home. What elements in its worship service most help you connect with and worship God? Have you noticed aspects of worship in other congregations that open spiritual pathways for you?
   - *Celebration*: Be happy in your faith as you go about your daily places! However, don't pretend as if you're happy if you're not; Christian faith isn't about pretending. Perceive God's presence as filling your life places, and be joyful about God's grace!
   - *Service*: Do you avoid certain people and places? Do your life's places function as a comfort zone for you? How can you break out of that zone to serve others? What talents do you have to offer God in service?

- *Prayer*: Paul says, "Devote yourselves to prayer, keeping alert in it with thanksgiving" (Col. 4:2). Make all your places a chance to pray silently.
- *Fellowship*: In the places of your life, which people build you up? Which people drag you down? Is it possible to reorganize your life so that you spend time with more "build up" people than "drag down" people?
- *Confession*: Who among your fellowship are trusted friends? Is your pastor someone to whom you can go with a problem? Survey your life places for people you can trust with problems and decisions. God can work wonderfully in such people.
- *Submission*: In the spiritual sense, this word doesn't mean being passive when others are aggressive or abusive. It means you're humble; you know yourself and your gifts but you're focused on God's will. How Christlike are you? How attuned are you right now to God's will? How are you "showing Christ" in your life places?

small-group guide

These prayers, discussion questions, and exercises can be used for individual or group study. Each set of questions takes ten to twenty minutes. If you are using this book with a group, select questions based upon your group's interests and needs. Also included are suggestions for additional activities and reading if you'd like to continue exploring some of the themes.

Each week, ask a different person to read the opening prayer and another person to read the study questions. Use these questions as written, or use them as jumping-off points for your discussion and reflection. Enjoy the process of spiritual discovery! Stay open to the spontaneity of the Holy Spirit.

Close with quiet time to pray.

chapter 1

Opening Prayer

Dear Lord, we're all on a life journey. As we've passed through the events and circumstances of our lives, we've experienced some wonderful places, some not-so-good, and some terrible. We haven't always recognized your presence during our journeys. We tend to forget about you when things go well, and we grow fearful and unsure of your grace when things go awry. Your footprints are unseen [Ps. 77:19]. Help us perceive your grace both now and in hindsight. Inspire our memories and our imaginations so that your goodness becomes clear to us, in Jesus' name. Amen.

Questions

1. Read all of Psalm 18, from which I take this book's title. Why is a "wide place" important for the psalmist? What is his situation? What did the Lord do to help him? When you hear the phrase, "[God] gave me a wide place," what images come to your mind?

2. Read Psalms 4, 18, 23, 118, and 121. As you read, quickly write down any images that come to your mind. How does your imagination portray God's wide places? Do you think about actual places in your experience? (For instance, when I read Psalm 18, I think of driving the windy U.S. 89 through the mountains of Arizona.) Do you think about imaginary places?

3. Read Matthew 7:13-14 (RSV). Contrast the psalmists' image of "the wide place" with Jesus' image of a narrow "way." What is the narrow way? How, paradoxically, is the narrow way a "wide place of grace"?

4. Read Psalm 139. Have you ever wanted "time out" from God? What is the psalmist's situation? What does the psalmist want from God? Is the psalmist grateful or chagrined that God fills every place?

Also read Psalm 42 and 43. What seems to be the psalmist's problem? Why does God seem absent? Has anyone ever asked you, "Where is your God?"

5. Read Genesis 28:10-22; Exodus 3:1-4:17; and Luke 24:13-35. What is the place described? How does God appear to these people? Would you say they were mature in their faith before God appeared to them? Do they learn right away or do they have to struggle to understand? What do they learn from the experience? Consider any similar places in your life where God made God's self known in an obvious or subtle way.

Have you ever asked God for a sign? Where were you at the time? What happened?

Closing Prayer

End your time with a prayer that God provide you guidance and insight as you continue this study. Lift up in prayer people you know who are struggling to know God. Ask God for guidance and help for the coming week.

Go a Little Deeper

* Look up *stone*, *rock*, and *refuge* in a biblical concordance. Study a few of those scriptures. What insights do you find concerning God?

* Study biblical places in a Bible dictionary. Start by just browsing through the text to see what places spark your interest. What places strike you?

* Read Robert M. Hamma, *Landscapes of the Soul: A Spirituality of Place* (Notre Dame, Ind.: Ave Maria Press, 1999).

* Many novelists and essayists write about place from a variety of perspectives: Wendell Berry, Gretel Ehrlich, Witold Rybczynski, Annie Dillard, Wallace Stegner, John Knoepfle, and others. Discover an author you particularly like.

chapter 2

Opening Prayer

Dear Lord, all of us have homes, both past and present. Even you: when you came and dwelled among us, you stayed at a place and invited disciples to visit with you [John 1:37-39]. All of us have different experiences of home, but you have been with us through all these experiences. Clarify for us the ways that your Spirit has guided us. If necessary, heal our emotions. Deepen our understanding and our integrity, that we might find balance and a strong "center" in you, in Jesus' name. Amen.

Questions

1. What is your home like? Do you have reminders of other places where you've lived? Do you have particular objects (a picture, china, and so on) that give you a sense of peace? What plants and animals live near your home? Do you consider yourself a hospitable person with your home, or is your home a private sanctuary?

Don't forget that spirituality doesn't necessarily involve inner peace and fulfillment. Spirituality includes conflict and struggle. Have you experienced God in your home in terms of struggle, problem solving, reconciliation? Has home been a safe haven or a place of anxiety for you? Compare your present home to your childhood home(s).

2. Do you have a place in your home where you feel especially peaceful and spiritual? It could be a room, a chair, even the bathtub! What makes that place special? Do you read devotional material or have some other kind of spiritual routine? If so, where do you go?

3. Discuss your roots. What places give you a sense of rootedness? Are they the same as the favorite and sacred places you already considered? How do you feel connected with God in those places? Do

you have contact with your root places? If not, could you plan a visit sometime soon?

4. Write your own "roots" faith statement based on Deuteronomy 26:4-5. Make it longer or shorter than those verses. Ask people to share their statement if they feel comfortable doing so.

5. What is the economic health of your community? Discuss in your group what ministry opportunities you perceive in your community. How do people need help? What aspects of your area need positive change?

Closing Prayer

Thank God for divine help in your life. Thank God for the special people in your life—past and present—whose home became your home-away-from-home. Lift up people you know who are struggling with an unsatisfactory home life. Ask God for guidance and assurance for the upcoming days.

Go a Little Deeper

* Obtain a topical Bible that categorizes scripture passages according to themes. Look up *providence* and study biblical passages that deal with God's care.

* Read Diana R. Garland, *Sacred Stories of Ordinary Families: Living the Faith in Daily Life* (San Francisco: Jossey-Bass, 2003).

chapter 3

Opening Prayer

Dear Lord, you've promised us abundant life. Too often we take abundant life for granted, if indeed we even understand what it is. But we do know what happiness is. We know what relief feels like when we relax or have fulfilled a goal or solved a major problem. We know the beauty of love when we feel the least loveable. We celebrate when we get a warning rather than a ticket! We feel wonderful freedom when we let go of a grudge, when our apologies are accepted, and when we're forgiven. Teach us new things about the life you give in Jesus' name. Amen.

Exercises

1. What does the phrase "abundant life" mean to you? Look up these verses: Rom. 5:8-11, 20-21; 6:23; 8:1-2, 31-39; 1 Cor. 6:9-11; 15:51-57; Gal. 3:27-29; Eph. 2:14-16; Phil. 2:5-8. What do these verses teach you, and how do they relate to the idea of abundant life?

2. To portray abundant life, Jesus uses images of a safe place (John 10:8-10). Imagine a sheepfold near everything a sheep needs: water, food, companionship (sheep dislike being solitary), and peace. Discuss the things that we need to make life worthwhile. You may think of food, clothing, shelter, companionship, beauty (in nature, music, and so on), and times and places for relaxing, laughter, and renewal. Discuss how these things are gifts from God.

3. After you read chapter 3, look up the verses that describe Paul's childlike qualities. What makes a Christian childlike (as opposed to childish)?

4. Read parables of Jesus: Matthew 13:1-52 and Luke 15:1-16:13 contain several well-known ones. Write your own parable: "The kingdom of heaven is like a . . ." Use an illustration from your childhood or adult experiences.

5. My friend Michael, who contributed a story of his love of the outdoors, also wrote a poem about one of his favorite places.

Mountain Creek Water Fall

water cycle creek
is spiritual
contact,
soothing balm to real experience,
piano riffs
of soul tinkling, flowing, traveling
to next display of joy
dance

cacophony of
splashing, slathering
water
over rocks and between, around
solid mass chunks
water music primal chord striking,
relaxing, soothing, setting
free

riotous and noisy
inner splash cascades
dissolve
selfish needs, fears, guilty secrets
’til mellow calm
pervades and soothing peaceful pooling,
flowing, swirling, calming
breathes

avalanching liquid

into sunlit voids
rumbles
creating sound symphony,
gravity awes
those aware intuit surrounding,
insightful, beckoning
God

stand bravely amidst
shimmering veil mists
soaring
experience familiar mystic
kiss of insight
discerning your call is to mirror
creative, nurturing
love

In your group, use Michael's poem as inspiration for your own poem about an outdoor place where you experience God's presence. Write the poem as it comes to you and then revise it later.

Closing Prayer

Thank God for happy places, whether they're "spiritually correct" or not! Thank God for the amusement park, for your yard, for the mall, for childhood places. Ask God to give you a fresh sense of God's divine presence and a renewed sense of joy. Pray for people who seem glum and unhappy.

Go a Little Deeper

* Look up *gate* in a Bible dictionary. What city gates are mentioned in the Bible? Did different gates have different public purposes? Can you think of a modern equivalent to the city gate?

* Read Donald E. Demaray, *Laughter, Joy, and Healing* (Grand

Rapids, Mich.: Baker Book House, 1986); Robert M. Hamma, *Earth's Echo: Sacred Encounters with Nature* (Notre Dame, Ind.: Ave Maria Press, 2002); or Jon Pahl, *Shopping Malls and Other Sacred Spaces: Putting God in Place* (Grand Rapids, Mich.: Brazos Press, 2003).

chapter 4

Opening Prayer

Dear Lord, you're the perfect place to go when we're in trouble. You're the one we turn to when things fall apart. You're a better dwelling place and refuge than even our favorite places! We remember places when trouble came our way. The entire place became sullied in memory; a nice community became "the place where I lost my job" or "the place where I was robbed" or associated with other unfortunate circumstances. Help us turn to you in times of joy and trouble alike. Heal our memories, whether by an outpouring of the Spirit, a helpful book, a verse of Scripture, or a trusted friend or counselor. In Jesus' name we pray. Amen.

Exercises

1. Read Psalm 77. What is the psalmist's situation? What has God done in the past? What gives the psalmist hope for the future?
2. Also read Psalms 22, 69, 73, and 90. What is the basis of the psalmists' hope? Does Psalm 90 express any hope at all? What other psalms do you turn to in time of trouble?
3. How do you respond in a spiritual way to illness? Do you ask people to pray for you? Do you "go it alone"? Do you have a pastor or chaplain visit you in the hospital? Discuss experiences when you've dealt with serious illness. Where were you? Does that place remain a reminder to you?

Look up several of Jesus' healing miracles in the New Testament. Where did they happen? Did Jesus heal anyone without their consent? How does Jesus heal people today?

4. What have been your "wilderness places" where you felt lost, at loose ends, and unsure of God's help? Did you remain strong in your faith? Did you grumble about God's faithfulness? Did your grumbling clear the air so that you felt stronger in your faith? What resolved that situation?

5. Read Luke 13:1-5 and James 4:13-15. What lessons does trouble teach us?

Closing Prayer

Thank God for healing! Understand that we all heal emotionally in different ways, and at different paces. Don't be discouraged if people insensitively say, "You need to move on," but don't wallow in your pain either. Ask God to show you the best way to deal with your hurt. Lift up people who struggle with tragedy and terrible memories.

Go a Little Deeper

* Read a good book that helps you deal with a problem or a hurt or general confusion! For instance, Robert Corin Morris, *Wrestling with Grace: A Spirituality for the Rough Edges of Daily Life* (Nashville, Tenn.: Upper Room Books, 2003); Joyce Rupp, *Praying Our Goodbyes* (Notre Dame, Ind.: Ave Maria Press, 1988); or Lewis B. Smedes, *Forgive and Forget: Healing the Hurts We Don't Deserve* (San Francisco: HarperCollins, 1984). Or browse the selections at your local bookstore.

* Study a history book that deals with a tragedy, for example, a book on the Holocaust or a natural disaster.

chapter 5

Opening Prayer

Lord, there are lots of churches around. Some have pretty buildings, some plain, but the most glorious church building can be a place of hurt feelings or the solution to our problems. The simplest little church can hold lots of trouble or abundant love. Give us discernment to understand our church places better. Give us honest insight into our own needs and hurts so we don't make trouble in our church places. If necessary, help us find a congregation that is a true fellowship. Help us learn love, forgiveness, and grace in our church place, in Christ's name. Amen.

Exercises

1. After you read chapter 5, study the qualities of churches as described by Paul. Look up the verses in the Bible to gain the context. How closely does your church conform to Paul's vision? How does it fall short?

2. Study the questions about congregations in chapter 5. How many can you answer off the top of your head? How healthy does your church seem to be?

3. Are you happy at your church? Why or why not? Make a "serenity prayer" list of things about your church: the things you can change (including yourself) and the things you cannot change, including a prayer for wisdom to know the difference.

4. Read 1 Corinthians 3. List qualities of leadership that are stated or implied in that chapter. Is Paul's vision for leadership different from other kinds? Could Paul run for public office and win?

5. First Corinthians 12–14 deals with spiritual gifts (even though chapter 13 is sometimes quoted separately as a prose-poem about the nature of love). Read those three chapters. What is a spiritual gift? Is it different from a talent? How does God want us to use these gifts?

Closing Prayer

Thank God for your life's churches. Ask God to keep those congregations faithful. Ask God to keep church leaders focused upon God's will. Ask God to help you grow spiritually at your church.

Go a Little Deeper

* Over the next several weeks, read Galatians and 1 and 2 Corinthians with the help of a commentary. What issues did Paul face in these churches? How does his advice apply today?

* Look through the several books listed in the notes section for chapter 5. There are a lot of books available concerning churches and church leadership. I haven't listed nearly all of them. Find a book title that interests you from among the end notes, obtain a copy from your local bookstore, and study the issues discussed there. Or browse the selections at your bookstore.

* Plan a fun event at your church. Have no purpose to the event except happiness and fellowship. Then plan more such events in the future.

chapter 6

Opening Prayer

Dear Lord, our lives are postcard scrapbooks of different locations. Some were home, and some were merely visited. Your presence touched us in all those locations, but we didn't always perceive it, nor did we understand the lasting effects of your grace. Like the biblical places we've studied, make our places continual reminders of your love. Help us draw strength from your great works of the past, that we might have faith for the present and the future, in Christ's precious name. Amen.

Exercises

1. Discuss what you've learned about "wide places of grace" from these readings and conversations. Do you perceive God's grace any differently? How do you answer the "where are you?" question from chapter 1?

2. Are you shy or confident as a Christian witness? How comfortable do you feel telling others about what God has done in your life? (Sometimes we feel self-conscious about appearing holier-than-thou or insensitive.)

3. How have you traditionally felt about spiritual disciplines? (1) "We're saved by grace and not works, so God should just 'zap' me without my efforts." (2) "I'm not nearly a good enough person to try spiritual exercises! Those are for preachers and monks!" (3) "I've tried them, but they're too much like New Year's resolutions." (4) "I've tried them and I'd like to keep some of the disciplines regularly."

4. Reread chapter 1, specifically the last three sections: "For I Will Not Leave You," "Holy Ground," and "On the Road." What do these encounters with God teach you about your own sacred places?

5. Memorize Psalm 18:36 and Psalm 31:7-8. Keep these verses in mind as you go about your daily tasks and places.

Closing Prayer

Thank God for one another. Ask God's continued blessings and guidance as you go about your life and your "religious adventures." Pray for me (the author) and people I know. Ask God's help as you consider other study books for your spiritual growth.

Go a Little Deeper

* We have read about several unusual biblical place names like YHWH Jireh ("the Lord will provide") and Beer-lahai-roi ("the well of the One who sees me"). Repeat exercise 1, chapter 2 (p. 64), but name your significant places in the style of those biblical names. Be

creative. Name a place "God helped me deal with a jerk," "God saved me when I failed," "God seemed to ignore me," "God sobered me up," "God gave me a best friend," "God gave me this place to return to," and so on. Memorialize those places in some way, perhaps by writing the names on a map or by placing stones in your garden.

notes

Introduction

1. Many books approach the sense of place from various angles: an extremely short list of available resources includes Yi-Fu Tuan, *Topophilia: A Study of Environmental Perception, Attitudes, and Values* (New York: Columbia University Press, 1974); Gaston Bachelard, *The Poetics of Space,* trans. Maria Jolas (Boston: Beacon Press, 1994), Edward S. Casey, *Getting Back into Place: Toward a Renewed Understanding of the Place-World* (Bloomington, Ind.: Indiana University Press, 1993); John R. Stilgoe, *Outside Lies Magic: Regaining History and Awareness in Everyday Places* (New York: Walker and Co., 1998); Paul G. Chamberlain, "Topomystica: Investigation into the Concept of Mystic Place," *Journal of Cultural Geography*, 10, no. 1 (Fall/Winter 2001:97–123; Timothy K. Beal, *Roadside Religion: In Search of the Sacred, the Strange, and the Substance of Faith* (Boston: Beacon Press, 2005). My thanks go to my friend, historian, and author Keith Sculle, who alerted me to some of these texts.

2. One classic study is Walter Brueggemann, *The*

Land: Place as Gift, Promise, and Challenge in Biblical Faith, 2nd ed. (Minneapolis, Minn.: Fortress Press, 2002). Brueggemann argues that the land is of central importance to understanding biblical faith (p. 3). See also a very comprehensive text by Menashe Har-El, *Landscape, Nature, and Man in the Old Testament: A Commentary on Biblical Sites and Events* (Jerusalem: Carta, 2003), which explains many specific locations mentioned in the Bible.

3. J. Clinton McCann Jr., "The Book of Psalms," in *The New Interpreter's Bible*, vol. 4 (Nashville, Tenn.: Abingdon Press, 1996), 697.

4. Albert M. Shulman, *Gateway to Judaism: Encyclopedia Home Reference* (South Brunswick, N.J.: Thomas Yoseloff, 1971), 1:300.

5. Marcus J. Borg, *The Heart of Christianity: Rediscovering a Life of Faith* (San Francisco: HarperSanFrancisco, 2003), 155–63.

Chapter 1

1. Tuan, *Topophilia*.

2. Philip Sheldrake, *Spaces for the Sacred: Place, Memory, and Identity* (Baltimore, Md.: Johns Hopkins University Press, 2001), 1.

3. Brueggemann, *The Land*, 4.

4. Sheldrake, *Spaces for the Sacred*, 7.

5. Frank McCourt, "Where We Pray," *Life* (December 10, 2004):11.

6. Surinder Mohan Bhardwaj, *Hindu Places of Pilgrimage in India: A Study in Cultural Geography* (Berkeley, Calif.: University of California Press, 1973).

7. Sheldrake, *Spaces for the Sacred*, 48–51.

8. For a good discussion of God's local v. universal presence, on which I've based these comments, see Walther Eichrodt, *Theology of the Old Testament,* trans. J. A. Baker (Philadelphia: Westminster Press, 1967), 2:186–94.

9. Shmuel Sambursky, *The Concept of Place in Late Neoplatonism* (Jerusalem: Israel Academy of Sciences and Humanities, 1982), 15, 35.

10. Max Jammer, *Concepts of Space: The History of Theories of Space in Physics*, 3rd ed. (New York: Dover Publications, 1993), 30.

11. Abraham E. Millgram, *Jewish Worship* (Philadelphia, Pa.: Jewish Publication Society of America, 1971), 289.

12. Quoted in Jammer, *Concepts of Space*, 31–32.

13. I obtained the phrase "religious adventure" from Millgram, *Jewish Worship*, 92.

14. Robert M. Hamma, *Landscapes of the Soul: A Spirituality of Place* (Notre Dame, Ind.: Ave Maria Press, 1999), 20.

15. Niles Elliot Goldstein, *God at the Edge: Searching for the Divine in Uncomfortable and Unexpected Places* (New York: Bell Tower, 2000), xi.

16. Dan Wakefield, *Spiritually Incorrect: Finding God in All the Wrong Places* (Woodstock, Vt.: Skylight Paths Publishing, 2004), 154.

17. James W. Moore, *If You're Going the Wrong Way . . . Turn Around!* (Nashville, Tenn.: Dimensions for Living, 2004).

18. Hamma, *Landscapes of the Soul*, 20–21.

19. Kathleen Norris, *Dakota: A Spiritual Geography* (Boston: Houghton Mifflin Co., 1993), 2.

20. W. Gunther Plaut, ed., *The Torah: A Modern Commentary* (New York: The Union of American Hebrew Congregations, 1981), 196.

21. Annie Dillard, *Teaching a Stone to Talk: Expeditions and Encounters* (New York: Harper & Row Publishers, 1982), 40.

22. Plaut, ed., *The Torah*, 407.

23. *Complete Poems of Robert Frost, 1949* (New York: Henry Holt and Co., 1949), 324.

24. Frederick Buechner, *The Magnificent Defeat* (New York: Seabury, 1966), 85–86, quoted in *The New Interpreter's Bible* (Nashville, Tenn.: Abingdon Press, 1995), 9:482.

Chapter 2

1. See, for instance, Elizabeth J. Canham, *Heart Whispers: Benedictine Wisdom for Today* (Nashville, Tenn.: Upper Room Books, 1999), chap. 5.

2. Hamma, *Landscapes of the Soul*, 79.

3. Diana R. Garland, *Sacred Stories of Ordinary Families: Living the Faith in Daily Life* (San Francisco: Jossey-Bass, 2003).

4. Ibid., 197. A cautionary discussion about household religion is found in Jon Pahl, *Shopping Malls and Other Sacred Places: Putting God in Place* (Grand Rapids, Mich.: Brazos Press, 2003), chap. 5.

5. Millgram, *Jewish Worship*, 290.

6. McCourt, "Where We Pray," 13.

7. Wendell Berry, "An Argument for Diversity," in *What Are People For?* (San Francisco: North Point Press, 1990), 109–22.

8. Emily Brontë, "Stanzas" at www.gutenberg.org/dirs/etext97/brntp10.txt

9. Bradley Shavit Artson, "Turning," in *Tikkun*, 17, no. 5 (Sept.–Oct. 2002), 66–67 (quotation from p. 66).

10. C. S. Lewis, *Surprised by Joy: The Shape of My Early Life* (New York: Harcourt, Brace & World, 1955), 16–18.

11. Henry David Thoreau, *Walden: or, Life in the Woods and On the Duty of Civil Disobedience* (New York: New American Library, 1960), 15.

12. Sheldrake, *Spaces for the Sacred*, 10.

13. Donald K. McKim, "Providence: A Genealogy," www.sblsite.org/Article.aspx?ArticleId=154. McKim cites the book by Benjamin Wirt Farley, *The Providence of God* (Grand Rapids, Mich.: Baker Book House, 1988) for a detailed study of the doctrine of providence.

14. Thomas Merton, *The Seven Storey Mountain* (New York: Signet Books, 1948), 412.

Chapter 3

1. This paragraph is adapted from my article "The Jesus Diet" in *The Christian Century* 120, no. 15 (July 26, 2003):19.

2. Donald E. Demaray, *Laughter, Joy, and Healing* (Grand Rapids, Mich.: Baker Book House, 1986), 198.

3. Ibid., 68.

4. The well-known piece was first published by Nadine Strain, misspelled *Stair*, in a 1978 issue of *Family Circle* magazine but has often been reprinted, according to Byron Crawford, *Kentucky Stories* (Paducah, Ky.: Turner Publishers, 1994), 1–2.

5. Maxie D. Dunnam, *Barefoot Days of the Soul* (Nashville, Tenn.: Upper Room Books, 1976).

6. Robert M. Hamma, *Earth's Echo: Sacred Encounters with Nature* (Notre Dame, Ind.: Ave Maria Books, 2002).

7. Crawford, *Kentucky Stories*, 108–9.

8. A version of the poem comes from www.contemplator.com/scotland/rowan.html.

9. Sheldrake, *Spaces for the Sacred*, 8–9. See also Jon Pahl's excellent discussions of American places in his book, *Shopping Malls and Other Sacred Places*, chap. 3 and throughout, and also Pete Ward, *God at the Mall: Youth Ministry That Meets Kids Where They're At* (Peabody, Mass.: Hendrickson Publishers, 1999).

10. Stephen Dobyns, *Velocities: New and Selected Poems, 1966-1992* (New York: Viking Penguin Books, 1994), 213–14.

11. Terence E. Fretheim, "The Book of Genesis," *The New Interpreter's Bible* (Nashville, Tenn.: Abingdon Press, 1994), 1:492.

12. Paul J. Achtemeier, ed., *The HarperCollins Bible Dictionary* (San Francisco: HarperSanFrancisco, 1996), 1091.

13. Merrill C. Tenney, ed., *The Zondervan Pictorial Bible Dictionary* (Grand Rapids, Mich.: Zondervan Publishing House, 1967), 300.

14. This section is also adapted from my piece "The Jesus Diet," 19.

Chapter 4

1. Tenney, ed., *The Zondervan Pictorial Bible Dictionary*, 894.

2. Brueggemann, *The Land*, 28.

3. Tenney, ed., *The Zondervan Pictorial Bible Dictionary*, 500.

4. Plaut, ed., *The Torah*, 111.

5. Ibid.

6. Ibid., 143.

7. Patrick D. Miller, "The Book of Jeremiah," *The New Interpreter's Bible*, 6:816.

8. Gerald L. Keown, Pamela J. Scalise, Thomas G. Smothers, *Jeremiah 26-52*, Word Biblical Commentary series (Nashville, Tenn.: Nelson Reference and Electronic Publishing, 1995), 27:17–18.

9. Keown et al., *Jeremiah 26-52*, 18.

Chapter 5

1. Stanley Hauerwas, "The Family as a School for Character," in Gabriel Palmer-Fernandez, comp., *Moral Issues: Philosophical and*

Religious Perspectives (Upper Saddle River, N.J.: Prentice Hall, 1996), 244.

2. Ibid.

3. I've developed these questions from my own experiences and also several excellent books that help ministers and churches identify their strengths and weaknesses. Such books include Herb Miller, *The Vital Congregation: Ten Basic Measurements* (Nashville, Tenn.: Abingdon Press, 1990); Lyle E. Schaller, *Looking in the Mirror: Self-Appraisal in the Local Church* (Nashville, Tenn.: Abingdon Press, 1984); William M. Easum, *The Church Growth Handbook* (Nashville, Tenn.: Abingdon Press, 1990); Loren B. Mead, *More Than Numbers: The Way Churches Grow* (Bethesda, Md.: Alban Institute, 1993); and others. Lyle E. Schaller, *The Interventionist* (Nashville, Tenn.: Abingdon Press, 1997), contains nearly four hundred diagnostic questions for churches. Also Iva Carruthers, ed., *Blow the Trumpet in Zion* (Minneapolis, Minn.: Fortress Press, 2005); Floyd Massey and Samuel Berry McKinney, *Church Administration in the Black Perspective* (Valley Forge, Pa.: Judson Press, 2003).

4. R. Paul Stevens and Phil Collins, *The Equipping Pastor: A Systems Approach to Congregational Leadership* (Bethesda, Md.: Alban Institute, 1993), 33, 76. I am indebted to this book and highly recommend it for anyone approaching issues of parish growth and leadership. See also Peter L. Steinke, *Healthy Congregations: A Systems Approach* (Bethesda, Md.: Alban Institute, 1996).

5. Corinne Ware, *Discover Your Spiritual Type: A Guide to Individual and Congregational Growth* (Bethesda, Md.: Alban Institute, 1995).

6. My essay "Leadership, Change, and the Parish," *The Quarterly Review* (Summer 1996):203–19, discusses these and related issues. Pastors have no dearth of texts on parish leadership; in fact, digesting such material amid the pressures of congregational leadership can be difficult. See, for example, Norman Shawchuck and Roger Heuser, *Leading the Congregation: Caring for Yourself while Serving the People* (Nashville, Tenn.: Abingdon Press, 1993) and their *Managing the Congregation: Building Effective Systems to Serve People* (Nashville, Tenn.: Abingdon Press, 1996); R. Robert Cueni, *What Ministers Can't Learn in Seminary: A Survival Manual for the Parish Ministry* (Nashville, Tenn.: Abingdon Press, 1988); Kennon L. Callahan, *Twelve Keys to an Effective Church* (San Francisco: Harper

SanFrancisco, 1983) and his *Effective Church Leadership: Building on the Twelve Keys* (San Francisco: HarperSanFrancisco, 1990); James D. Anderson and Ezra E. Jones, *The Management of Ministry: Building Leadership in a Changing World* (Nashville, Tenn.: Discipleship Resources, 1993); and many others.

7. Stevens and Collins, *The Equipping Pastor*, 9.

8. Ibid., chaps. 4 and 5. See also Anne Messer, *Contemporary Images of Christian Ministry* (Nashville, Tenn.: Abingdon Press, 1989); Thomas P. Sweetser and Carol W. Holden, *Leadership in a Successful Parish* (San Francisco: HarperSanFrancisco, 1986); Bernard F. Swain, *Liberating Leadership: Practical Styles of Pastoral Ministry* (San Francisco: HarperSanFrancisco, 1986).

9. Shawchuck and Heuser name three keys to change within congregations: anticipation (the ability to see the congregation's spiritual and organizational "seasons"), innovation (the ability to help the congregation do things better than in the past), and excellence (a commitment to quality). *Leading the Congregation*, 167–81. James O'Toole, in his book *Leading Change: Overcoming the Ideology of Comfort and the Tyranny of Custom* (Somerset, N.J.: Jossey-Bass, 1995), offers no fewer than thirty-three hypotheses to account for resistance to change.

Lyle E. Schaller's several books about change include *The Change Agent: The Strategy of Innovative Leadership* (1972), *Strategies for Change* (1993), and *The Interventionist* (1997), all published by Abingdon Press. See also C. Jeff Woods, *We've Never Done It Like This Before: 10 Creative Approaches to the Same Old Church Tasks* (Bethesda, Md.: Alban Institute, 1994). Michael G. Fullan also writes perceptively about organizational change in *Change Forces: Probing the Depths of Educational Reform* (Philadelphia, Pa.: Taylor & Francis, 1993). See also William M. Easum, *Dancing with Dinosaurs: Ministry in a Hostile and Hurting World* (Nashville, Tenn.: Abingdon Press, 1993), and *Sacred Cows Make Gourmet Burgers: Ministry Anytime, Anywhere, by Anyone* (Nashville, Tenn.: Abingdon Press, 1995).

10. Lorraine Kisly, ed., *Ordinary Graces: Christian Teachings on the Interior Life* (New York: Bell Tower, 2000), 192.

11. Marcus J. Borg discusses Christian practices as "thin places" in

his book *The Heart of Christianity: Rediscovering a Life of Faith* (San Francisco: HarperSanFrancisco, 2003), 157–61.

12. G. C. Berkouwer, *The Providence of God: Studies in Dogmatics* (Grand Rapids, Mich.: Wm. B. Eerdmans Publishing Co., 1952), 223.

13. Ibid., 225–26.

14. Roland H. Bainton, *Here I Stand: A Life of Martin Luther* (New York: New American Library, 1950), 287.

15. Paul Althaus, *The Theology of Martin Luther*, trans. Robert C. Schultz (Philadelphia, Pa.: Fortress Press, 1966), 353.

16. Some denominations have additional sacraments, of course. Churches also disagree on how they define Christ's presence in the Eucharist, whether as a literal transformation or a spiritual presence, with many theological nuances.

17. This section is slightly adapted from my article "Joined at the Heart" in *The Christian Century* 120, no. 15 (July 26, 2003):18.

Chapter 6

1. Dallas Willard, *The Spirit of the Disciplines: Understanding How God Changes Lives* (San Francisco: Harper & Row Publishers, 1988), 158–91.

about the author

DR. PAUL E. STROBLE is an elder of the Illinois Great Rivers Conference of The United Methodist Church. He has served both as parish pastor and college instructor and currently teaches at the University of Akron, where he earned an Excellence in Teaching award. He has been a writer-researcher for the United Methodist curriculum *FaithLink*, a long-time contributor to *Springhouse* magazine, and author of numerous articles, essays, poems, and curricular materials. Among his eleven books are the Abingdon titles *Paul and the Galatians* (2000), *Mystery: Experiencing the Mystery of God* (2002), *What Do Other Faiths Believe?* (2003), and *What Can I Believe About Science and Religion?* (2007). He is married to Dr. Beth Stroble, and they have a daughter, Emily.

Other Titles of Interest from UPPER ROOM BOOKS

An Eclectic Almanac for the Faithful: People, Places, and Events That Shape Us
W. Paul Jones
978-0-8358-9849-0

Leading a Life with God: The Practice of Spiritual Leadership
Daniel Wolpert
978-0-8358-1003-6

A Mile in My Shoes: Cultivating Compassion
Trevor Hudson
978-0-8358-9815-6

Provocative Grace: The Challenge in Jesus' Words
Robert Corin Morris
978-0-8358-9848-2